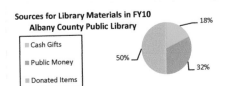

Sources for Library Materials in FY10
Albany County Public Library

- Cash Gifts
- Public Money
- Donated Items

18%

50%

32%

THE INVESTOR'S MANIFESTO

PREPARING FOR PROSPERITY, ARMAGEDDON, AND EVERYTHING IN BETWEEN

WILLIAM J. BERNSTEIN

WILEY

John Wiley & Sons, Inc.

Published by John Wiley & Sons, Inc., Hoboken, New Jersey.
Published simultaneously in Canada.

For general information on our other products and services or for technical
support, please contact our Customer Care Department within the United States
at (800) 762-2974, outside the United States at (317) 572-3993 or fax (317)
572-4002.

Wiley also publishes its books in a variety of electronic formats. Some content that
appears in print may not be available in electronic books. For more information
about Wiley products, visit our web site at www.wiley.com.

Library of Congress Cataloging-in-Publication Data:

Bernstein, William J.
    The investor's manifesto : preparing for prosperity, Armageddon, and
everything in between / William J. Bernstein.
        p.   cm.
    Includes bibliographical references and index.
    ISBN 978-0-470-50514-4 (cloth)
        1. Investments.   2. Securities.   3. Stocks.   4. Risk.   I. Title.
HG4521.B4456 2009
332.6—dc22

                                                            2009020116

Printed in the United States of America

10   9   8   7   6   5   4   3   2

To Kate, Johanna, and Max:
May they find this useful.

Contents

Foreword

Bill Bernstein—investment advisor, neurologist, economic historian, bestselling author, thinking person's financial guru—is perhaps the smartest man I know. And, fortunately, he is also one of the most approachable. Indeed, during my 13 years as the *Wall Street Journal's* personal-finance columnist, he was the source I invariably turned to when the well ran dry.

"So, Bill, what's on your mind these days?" I would croon down the telephone, hoping a certain jocularity would mask my desperation as yet another column deadline loomed. Bill, thank goodness, almost always delivered. Because he had turned his considerable intelligence to the financial world relatively late in life, he had enthusiasm and insights that eluded the rest of us, who had grown jaded from watching the Wall Street money-go-round for too long.

You will discover that enthusiasm and those insights in *The Investor's Manifesto*, delivered in plain English and with a touch of hyperbole and a helping of humor. Bill and I do not agree on everything, but there is one thing we are both convinced of: The recent economic and market debacle is a great "teachable moment," to steal Bill's phrase from the preface, and it may represent the best investment opportunity in a generation.

So what should you learn from the 2008–2009 financial collapse? You will get Bill's take in the pages that follow. To get you warmed up, here I highlight five important—but perhaps less obvious—lessons.

1. Many of us are not as brave as we thought.

To earn high returns, we need to take high risks. The stock market sure seems risky in 2009, which is a reason for optimism. But even if stocks deliver healthy gains over the next few years, we may not reap the reward if we make panicky decisions in the face of market turmoil.

Have you got what it takes to be a successful stock-market investor? This may be the best chance you will ever get to assess your stomach for risk. If you calmly rode out the 2008–2009 decline, maybe you can indeed live with a stock-heavy portfolio. But if you were terrified by both the economic turmoil and your own investment losses, perhaps you should move toward a more conservative investment mix in the years ahead.

2. Leverage can sting.

Many of us engage in mental accounting, associating the auto loan with the car, the mortgage with the house, and the credit-card balance with the wild weekend in Cancun. Yet, once we have incurred these debts, they effectively leverage our entire finances. This simple truth has lately been hammered home, as the past decade's borrowing binge ran smack into the brutal decline in stock and home prices.

Let's say you went into 2008 with a $400,000 house, a $200,000 stock portfolio, and $300,000 in debts. Your stock portfolio's value might have tumbled to $100,000 and your home might have dropped to $350,000, for a stinging 25 percent decline in your combined assets. But what really stung was the hit to your net worth, which is your total assets minus your total liabilities. That would have fallen a staggering 50 percent.

3. Our homes likely will not pay for our retirement.

The recent collapse in the housing market should have finally killed off the popular notion that "you can't go wrong with real estate." Even if folks are no longer banking on double-digit annual housing gains, they often still view their homes as part of their retirement nest eggs.

To be sure, upon quitting the work force, we could unlock some of our home equity by trading down to a smaller place or taking out a reverse mortgage. But buying and selling real estate is not cheap, and reverse mortgages come loaded with fees. Moreover, we have to live somewhere—which means our homes are best viewed as a consumption item, not as an investment.

4. We need to save. Duh.

If we cannot bank on double-digit annual housing gains—or, for that matter, double-digit stock-market gains—what should we do? That's an easy one: We probably ought to be saving like crazy.

Indeed, with any luck, the recent economic turmoil will nix some of the silly justifications for America's pitifully low savings rate. In the 1990s, financial experts told us we did not need to save because our stock portfolios had grown so fat. In the current decade, experts assured us we did not need to save because our homes were worth so much.

Since then, of course, our stock portfolios and our homes have plummeted in value. It turns out the fabulous stock returns of the 1990s, and the glorious real-estate results of earlier this decade, were effectively borrowing from the future—and that future arrived with stomach-churning ferocity. The lesson: Do not use great investment returns as an excuse to cut back your savings rate, because great returns may be followed by wretched ones.

5. Perhaps the smart money is not so smart.

The earlier part of this decade was a time of great financial envy, as we watched the "smart money" buy into hedge funds, private equity, and other investments that were beyond the reach of ordinary investors. We imagined that they were getting mouth-watering returns, while we were left to invest in mundane mutual funds. Glorious returns? Alas, it did not turn out that way for those who invested with Bernie Madoff and his ilk.

But that is enough from me. It is time to listen to Bill. The odds are, you will be wiser for his words—and maybe wealthier, too.

Jonathan Clements
Author, *The Little Book of Main Street Money*
July 2009

Preface

I wrote my last investment book almost eight years ago, and I swore I would never write another. That was for two reasons.

The first was that finance is a relatively circumscribed field; not that much is really known for certain. The body of knowledge that the individual investor, or even the professional, needs to master is pitifully small. If most finance academics were asked to compile a body of truly essential scholarly articles, their lists would generally not be more than several dozen long. On the other hand, put the average doctor, social worker, or scientist to that task, and the required reading would fill many shelves, if not whole rooms. In short, I had said most of what I needed to say about finance in my first two books. Until now.

The financial meltdown of 2008–2009 drastically changed the investment landscape, and if there ever was a time to leapfrog my previous books, it is now. This is a teachable moment, and I intend to use it to clearly and concisely enunciate a set of timeless investment principles.

In 1934, the father of the science of modern value investing, Benjamin Graham, wrote a great brick of a book, *Security Analysis*, which spelled out today's commonly accepted techniques for evaluating stocks and bonds, and it remains to this day required reading for anyone seriously interested in finance. As with any comprehensive, variegated work, it strikes individual readers in different ways.

Graham's graceful prose and methodical composition bowled me over, a shining exemplar for any financial writer. He illuminated a devastated investment terrain of the battered stocks and bonds of the nation's once-mighty corporations strewn about and nearly available for the taking—in short, an environment not unlike today's.

Graham, almost alone among his generation of investors, ran the numbers and concluded that anyone with cash to spare was crazy *not* to own at least some stocks. He recommended a 50/50 stock/bond split; today, most would consider this allocation conservative, but in 1934 it struck most as certifiably reckless.

When I first read *Security Analysis* decades ago, Graham's descriptions of those chaotic long-ago markets reminded me of a B-movie about the Fall of Rome: faintly interesting, but hardly relevant to the placid and modern financial scene.

I was wrong—dead wrong. The markets are placid no longer, and at some points in 2008 and 2009 the resemblance of valuations to those of 1934 were closer than most of us would have liked; in the not-too-distant future, they may yet be again. As in the depths of the Great Depression, there are now generous returns to be had for the brave, the disciplined, and the liquid. If there was ever a time to own a prudent portfolio that includes equities for the long term, it is now.

My second reason for not wanting to consider another finance book had more to do with ideology than financial economics. Successful investing requires a skill set that very few people possess. This is difficult for me to admit; after all, I have written two books premised on the idea than anyone, given the proper tools, can turn the trick.

Once again, I was wrong. Having emailed and spoken to thousands of investors over the years, I have come to the sad conclusion that only a tiny minority will ever succeed in managing their money even tolerably well.

Successful investors need four abilities. First, they must possess an interest in the process. It is no different from carpentry, gardening, or parenting. If money management is not enjoyable, then a lousy job inevitably results, and, unfortunately, most people enjoy finance about as much as they do root canal work.

Second, investors need more than a bit of math horsepower, far beyond simple arithmetic and algebra, or even the ability to manipulate a spreadsheet. Mastering the basics of investment theory requires an understanding of the laws of probability and a working knowledge of statistics. Sadly, as one financial columnist explained to me more than a decade ago, fractions are a stretch for 90 percent of the population.

Third, investors need a firm grasp of financial history, from the South Sea Bubble to the Great Depression. Alas, as we shall soon see, this is something that even professionals have real trouble with.

Even if investors possess all three of these abilities, it will all be for naught if they do not have a fourth one: the emotional discipline to execute their planned strategy faithfully, come hell, high water, or the apparent end of capitalism as we know it. "Stay the course": It sounds so easy when uttered at high tide. Unfortunately, when the water recedes, it is not.

I expect no more than 10 percent of the population passes muster on each of the above counts. This suggests that as few as one person in ten thousand (10 percent to the fourth power) has the full skill set. Perhaps I am being overly pessimistic. After all, these four abilities may not be entirely independent: if someone is smart enough, it is also more likely he or she will be interested in finance and be driven to delve into financial history.

But even the most optimistic assumptions—increase the odds at any of the four steps to 30 percent and link them— suggests that no more than a few percent of the population is qualified to manage their own money. And even with the requisite skill set, more than a little moxie is involved. This last requirement—the ability to deploy what legendary investor Charley Ellis calls "the emotional game"—is completely independent of the other three; Wall Street is littered with the bones of those who knew just what to do, but could not bring themselves to do it.

As recently as a generation or two ago, lack of financial ability did not greatly handicap the average person. Most Americans did not have much money to invest, and the employees of large firms often participated in a traditional corporate defined-benefit (DB) pension plan, which was professionally managed and strove to provide them and their survivors with a reliable stream of retirement income.

The traditional DB plan, unfortunately, has gone the way of disco as Americans have had to become their own investment managers, herded like cattle into so-called defined-contribution (DC) plans—401(k)s, 403(b)s, and, worst of all, 457s. Somehow, the powers that be have decided that average workers should manage their own investments.

This makes about as much sense as expecting the average person to be his or her own airline pilot or family surgeon. Preposterous? Perhaps with flying complex aircraft or removing a son or daughter's appendix, but when it comes to managing retirement portfolios, most Americans find themselves in precisely this situation.

In fact, any reasonably intelligent person can solo a simple aircraft after a dozen hours of instruction, and surgeons occasionally joke that they could teach an above-average chimpanzee to perform an uncomplicated appendectomy. (The hard part is not knowing how, but rather, when to operate, and how to manage the patient before and after the surgery.) Yet, as the recent financial maelstrom demonstrates, competently and safely managing money often eludes even those at the pinnacle of the financial profession.

As a result, this book is fraught with a great deal of cognitive dissonance. I love investing and derive no small pleasure writing about it for others. Certainly, in a world where everyone has become his or her own investment manager, whether he or she likes it or not, helping small investors to manage their nest eggs would seem to be a laudable goal. It is just that it is not, in many cases, a realistic one.

That said, given current market conditions, I could not resist taking yet another stab at writing an easily comprehensible finance book. Certainly, I did not succeed with my first, *The Intelligent Asset Allocator*. I was gratified with the response to it, both among academics and general readers. Sadly, I was less than pleased by what my friends and family told me, which usually went something like this: "Jeez, Bill, it seems you know what you're talking about, but I fell sound asleep by the second chapter." So I wrote my second book, *The Four Pillars of Investing*, which I aimed, or so I thought, at the average liberal arts graduate. This time, I got fewer complaints, but there was still plenty of grousing about the unnecessary complexity of my tables, graphs, and examples.

This time around, I have attempted a book that I hope will be accessible to almost everyone, particularly the tens of millions who have found themselves unwillingly thrust into the role of portfolio manager. Rather than completely eliminate some of the more abstruse points, I have segregated them into optional boxed "Math Details," sections for more mathematically inclined readers that, while not essential, refine the appreciation of the investing process.

The Roadmap

This book's first three chapters explore the theoretical basis of investing and designing portfolios and are liberally laced with a fair amount of financial history. I have done this for two reasons. First, the theory can get pretty complex. Human beings deal with complexity by spinning narratives around it; this not only makes the difficult concepts more understandable, but also more entertaining as well. (Albert Einstein most famously resorted to piquant narrative to explain his theory of relativity by imagining the relative motion experienced by riders on two trains on parallel tracks. He did this not only to amuse and educate others, but also, at least initially, to help himself think about the process.)

Second, and more importantly, no matter how well an investor masters the theory of investing, he or she is lost if he or she lacks the ability to coolly observe extraordinary current events and say "I've seen this movie before, and I know how it ends." A small example will suffice: In 1994, former Salomon Brothers executive John Meriwether assembled the most brilliant group of financial experts ever seen, including Nobelists Myron Scholes and Robert Merton, into a firm called Long-Term Capital Management. Not only did his partners understand the mathematics behind their options-related strategies as well as anyone on Wall Street, but they were in many cases the inventors of these techniques.

For a few years, their strategies worked like a charm and generated annual returns of over 40 percent. There was just one problem: The data they based their strategies on covered only a relatively brief period of time. It never occurred to them to consider the longer span of data or the broad narrative sweep of financial history. Had they done so, they would have realized that about once every decade the wheels come completely off the machinery of the markets, and the old relationships among various kinds of investments, which they profited so mightily from, temporarily reverse with a vengeance.

In 1997 the world economy, along with Long-Term Capital Management, ran into a speed bump when Asia suffered from a debt crisis similar to the recent meltdown. The next year this spread to Russia, which defaulted on some of its debt. Around the world, the prices of nearly all financial assets, save those of the government bonds of developed nations, plummeted in unison—something that had not occurred during the brief period of market history that the Long-Term Capital partners had based their strategy on—and forced the company's liquidation under the anxious eyes of the Federal Reserve. Meriwether and his brilliant associates had made the classic mistake of getting their math right and their history wrong.

The present investment landscape is in many ways as extraordinary as any seen in finance, but its outlines are still easily understandable by those with a good grasp of the calumnies that have savaged investors in previous centuries. For example, anyone familiar with the collapse of Long-Term Capital Management would not have been taken completely by surprise by the recent meltdown. The point is not to predict when such calamities can occur—that is impossible—but simply to know that they *will* occur from time to time, and that you should design your long-term investment strategy appropriately.

If the financial disasters described in Chapters 1 and 2 do not convince you of the need to diversify your risks, then nothing will. In Chapter 3, I explore the ways in which ordinary investors can construct portfolios that should at least blunt some of the damage that can be rained down by the fickle goddess of finance.

Just as I employ a financial telescope to survey broad swaths of investment history and theory in the first three chapters, in the fourth a microscope turns inward to understand the greatest enemy facing investors: the visage in the mirror staring back at them.

The reason why most people do such lousy jobs with their portfolios is that human nature is an agar dish that breeds all manner of investing psychopathology. Two of the most virulent behavioral organisms are overconfidence and an overemphasis on recent history.

In 1998, a classic article by *Wall Street Journal* reporter Greg Ip dissected both these foibles. The Gallup organization polled investors in both June and September of that year—just before and just after the aforementioned Russian bond default and the Long-Term Capital Management debacle—on what they thought their own portfolio returns, and that of the overall market, would be.[1] Here were the results:

Expected Returns	June 1998	September 1998
Next year, own portfolio	15.2%	12.9%
Next year, overall U.S. market	13.4%	10.5%

Three things leap out from this table. First, note how optimistic the estimated returns are. These numbers are more than a bit higher than the long-term returns for stocks in the United States, the nation with the best results among all major markets.

Next, on average the individuals polled expected that they would beat the market by about 2 percent (the difference between the numbers in the first and second rows). This is remarkable, since, in the aggregate, these investors *are* the market. Further, average investors do not receive even the market return, but rather that return reduced by the expenses they pay. Within a few decades, these slow leaks will deflate any portfolio.

Finally, and most remarkably, their return estimates *fell* after that summer's price decline. Now, there is no greater truism in investing than this: The less you pay for an asset, the more money you are likely to make when you eventually sell it. A fall in price, under most circumstances, should lead to a higher expected return. Yet, the Gallup data quoted by Mr. Ip showed just the opposite: The average investor expects a higher return when buying at high prices than when buying at low ones.

Not only were American investors ludicrously over-confident, but their outlook was irrationally influenced by recent returns. Their estimates were grossly inflated by the high returns of the 1990s tech bubble, in which anyone who could fog a mirror could earn, at least for a little while, 20 percent per year.

Unfortunately, the long-term data on market returns showed 10 percent to be normal. Worse, the most commonly accepted methods for estimating future market returns suggested yet lower returns. Worst of all, investors' estimates moved in the *same* direction as stock prices, which is the opposite of what simple logic suggests.

Chapters 5 and 6 focus on dealing with the investment industry to execute the investment strategies devised in the previous chapters. Once you have mastered investment theory, investment history, and your own emotions, this is by far the easiest task.

I emphasize three main principles: first, to not be too greedy; second, to diversify as widely as possible; and third, to always be wary of the investment industry. People do not seek employment in investment banks, brokerage houses, and mutual fund companies with the same motivations as those who choose to work in fire departments or elementary schools. Whether investors know it or not, they are engaged in an ongoing zero-sum, life-and-death struggle with piranhas, and if rigorous precautions are not taken, the financial services industry will strip investors of their wealth faster than they can say "Bernie Madoff."

Consider this book a lifeboat manual. Tens of millions of Americans, and hundreds of millions abroad, have been tossed onto a turbulent investment sea. The waters are more dangerous than they have been in living memory, but, by the perverse calculus of finance, they should also be more rewarding. I hope that what readers learn here will help them make it to shore.

William J. Bernstein
North Bend, Oregon

CHAPTER

A Brief History of Financial Time

Many of life's deepest questions, I have found, get asked over lunch.

This particular midday meal occurred in 2000 at a Chinese restaurant in Manhattan, and my companion was a well-known hedge-fund manager and contributor to the academic finance literature. We puzzled, as did many in finance at the time, over the historically high prices of stocks.

"What I cannot figure out," my friend began, "is whether investors are really smart or really stupid." Seeing my puzzled expression, he continued, "Maybe the equity risk premium is still high, in which case prices will mean revert, which means that stock investors are really stupid. Alternatively, the equity risk premium has gotten a lot lower in the past 10 years, in which case prices will not mean revert, which means stock investors are really smart." Just what did he mean, and why was his question so important?

Since my friend is really smart and has worked in finance all his adult life, I have to translate his question into plain English: "In the past, stocks have had high returns because they have been really risky. But stocks are now so expensive that there are only two possibilities: either they are going to fall dramatically in price and then have higher returns after that (in which case investors are stupid for paying such high prices now), or there will be no big fall in price and little risk, but returns will hereafter be permanently low (in which case investors are smart). So which is it?"

We both knew that the intelligence or lack thereof on the part of investors, from the humblest 401(k) participant to the titans of finance, was of secondary importance. Rather, my friend's question cut to the heart of the nature of investing: the interplay between risk and return.

Sometime in the mid-1990s, people forgot about the risk/return nexus, and although the tech collapse of 2000–2002 briefly roused investors from their complacency, the damage was not deep enough, wide enough, or long enough to leave a lasting impression.

By contrast, by 2009 investors were fully aware of financial risk; whether they remain awake to its nature for another generation, as they did after the market collapse of 1929–1932, or for less than a year, as they did after 2002, remains to be seen. However long the current turmoil lasts, it provides an opportunity to explore a radically altered investing environment. This book focuses primarily on the critical relationship between risk and return and what it means to investors in the current turbulent environment.

In the Beginning

In order to understand the story of risk and return, we need to travel back to the dawn of civilization. We can divide the millennia-old saga of investing into three parts: the development of loan capital; the development of equity, or stock capital; and the development of the capital markets themselves.

From the beginning of human civilization, consumers have bought products from farmers and merchants, and all three have needed to borrow. In fact, the very first decipherable cuneiform clay tablets found in Mesopotamia, in what is now Iraq, primarily recorded production and business activity, and much of it consisted of credit transactions. Ordinary people often required credit to purchase food and shelter; farmers needed credit to buy seeds, tools, and both slave and hired labor; and merchants craved capital to outfit their trading expeditions with pack animals, ships, crew, trade goods, and currency.

Like any other commodity, money has its price. What we recognize as "money"—stamped silver, gold, and copper disks—would not be invented until the late seventh century B.C. by the Lydians in Asia Minor. But no matter. Almost any widely traded commodity can fill the bill, and for thousands of years before the invention of coins, grain, silver ingots, and cattle served as capital that could be loaned by creditors and borrowed by debtors.

To the ancient farmer, a bushel of seed grain or a head of cattle was capital enough. He could borrow them in one season and repay them, usually twice over, the next, a practice still observed in present-day primitive agricultural societies. At the origins of human agriculture, this investment return, referred to interchangeably as the "cost of capital" or the "interest rate," was 100 percent per growing season.

Why this very high rate of return? It happened for at least two reasons. The first was supply and demand. So poor were ancient agricultural societies, so great was their demand for capital, and so little was the excess of it available for lending, mainly in the hands of wealthy farmers and businessmen, that the possessors of capital could demand a sky-high price for it. The second factor that drove up the cost of capital was that all loans were considered risky. In those days, an equivalent of the risk-free Treasury bill (T-bill) did not exist, and every loan probably carried with it a significant probability of default. Not until the late medieval period did northern European governments begin to offer very secure "risk-free" notes and bills.

Which of these two factors—supply and demand or default risk—was the primary cause of the high rates? In my opinion, the supply/demand imbalance was the dominant one. Lenders have always demanded collateral in case of default, and in the ancient world, it could be draconian: the seizure of all of the debtor's property, or even his and his family's enslavement. These extreme measures offered lenders reasonable protection against default, and thus increased the supply of capital available to poor borrowers. Legislation that favors borrowers over creditors makes the latter less liable to lend, often causing more ultimate harm than good to the borrower; this is the essential tradeoff of bankruptcy law.

Over the centuries, with the gradual increase in wealth, capital became more abundant, and so its price—the rate of interest—fell. In the third millennium B.C., Sumerian borrowers paid 33 percent per year for loans of grain and 20 percent for loans of silver. A millennium later, the best Babylonian debtors borrowed silver at 10 percent. A millennium after that, the Greeks paid interest rates as low as 6 percent, and at the height of the Roman Empire, they fell as low as 4 percent.[1]

Just why have I spent the past few pages discussing this ancient history? After all, this is a book about modern-day investing. *Because for every consumer of capital, there is, more or less, a provider of capital.* That is where you, the investor—the provider of capital—come into the story. In the jargon of finance, the "cost of capital" to its consumers is exactly the same as the return to the investor, and as an investor, only by understanding the risks and rewards of the consumers of your capital can you truly understand the process.

So far, I have been dealing with what is known in the modern era as "debt financing." But throughout history, capital has also been supplied on another basis, which is through actual ownership shares, known today as "equity financing," in which the owner of excess capital gives it to the businessman or merchant in exchange for a share of the assets and future profits of the venture.

From the merchant or borrower's perspective, this is less risky than borrowing; if the merchant's venture fails, then he owes nothing beyond the investor's share of the residual assets of the venture, since there are no profits to distribute. But from the lender's perspective, providing equity capital is risky indeed, since he can lose capital more easily than with a loan.

Further, the equity investor finds it devilishly hard to calculate the potential upside of an equity investment; it might be astronomical, it might be puny, or it might be lost entirely. In the modern world, most large firms gather both debt capital from banks or from bond issuance and equity capital from shareholders. The lenders of capital—the banks and bondholders—are paid off first. Only then do the equity shareholders—the "residual owners"—get what remains.

> The stock shareholder is last in line to receive the payoff from a business. This is a risky proposition, and thus deserves a higher return, *on average*, than that earned by the bondholders, who get their money back first.

For these three reasons—the increased possibility of loss, the difficulty of estimating future profits, and the residual nature of equity ownership—a substantial return premium *should* be demanded by equity owners. This is the "equity risk premium" that my friend and I puzzled over that day at lunch.

Because of the risks of equity ownership, it did not develop on a large scale until relatively late in history. True, since ancient times small enterprises often spread ownership among individuals, but the first joint stock companies did not see light of day until the medieval period. Around A.D. 1150, a water mill in Bazacle in southern France divided its ownership into shares. When the Paris Bourse opened in the eighteenth century, these shares traded actively until 1946, when that nation's socialist government, apparently lacking a sense of economic history, nationalized the company.[2]

Around A.D. 1600, two much larger ventures, the English and Dutch East India Companies (hereafter referred to as the EIC and VOC, respectively, the latter by its Dutch initials), sold shares in their trading ventures, which were initially aimed at exploiting the fabulously profitable East Asian spice trade. The differences between the two companies spoke volumes about the power, wealth, and sophistication of these two nations, and about how investors were, and are, rewarded.

At that time, England was a backward, weak nation with almost no functioning capital markets. Queen Elizabeth I, who issued the EIC's charter, was, by modern standards, a corrupt monarch whose revenue came mainly from rents on royal lands and the sale of monopolies to court favorites (most famously, the sweet wine franchise to Sir Walter Raleigh). Lenders to the crown demanded high interest rates to compensate for the risk that monarchs could, and frequently did, renounce their debts at will.

Consequently, the cost of capital, that is, interest rates, in Tudor England were high. The lowest rates to high-quality borrowers with generous collateral were in the 10 to 14 percent range, while loan rates to riskier ventures and the crown were higher still.[3] The EIC, an even more uncertain enterprise, could not borrow capital at any price, nor could it even sell conventional shares. Instead, it was forced to offer fractional ownership in each annual expedition, return all of the investor's capital when the company's spice-laden ships returned from the East Indies, then raise capital all over again for the next expedition. Simply put, the EIC lacked permanent capital to sustain ongoing operations.

Fortunately for its investors, the EIC expeditions proved hugely successful, often paying returns in excess of 100 percent. Always remember, investment return and the cost of capital for business ventures are flip sides of the same coin. These very high returns meant that British business ventures paid dearly for their seed cash; this is not the way to grow an economy or make a nation powerful.

By contrast, the Dutch East India Company thrived in the Netherlands' sophisticated and trusted capital markets. By the late sixteenth century, its larger provincial governments and the best private borrowers got their capital at just 4 percent annual interest. When the VOC floated its stock shares, it was as permanent capital. The money was the company's to spend as it saw fit, and investors did not expect to see the initial investment back any time soon, beyond a regular stream of profits as dividends.

Dutch capital markets, with relatively low returns, a safer investment climate, and low-rate loans with which to fuel the nation's entrepreneurs, presented the mirror image to those in England, where investors earned higher returns, but only at the price of higher risk.

We now have two of the three elements in place needed to answer my friend's plaintive lunchtime question in the year 2000: debt and equity capital, and the difference between the costs of the two, the *equity risk premium*. In order to give us some idea of what to expect in terms of risk and return, all that is needed is an appreciation of the markets where they trade.

That debt and equity capital exist does not necessarily mean markets for them also do. The loan of a bushel of grain by one farmer to another in Mesopotamia in 2500 B.C. remained simply an agreement between these two men. Yes, the loan could be counted as an asset on the part of the lender, but it could not be easily sold by him to another investor. Likewise, until the establishment of the Paris Bourse, the owner of a share in the Bazacle mill could not easily sell it to someone else, although apparently, shares were occasionally traded among private individuals.

Near-Death in Venice

The real story of the capital markets begins in the fifth century A.D., when the collapse of the Roman Empire in the west drove a small group of refugees to seek shelter. They found it in an island group situated in an obscure lagoon nestled in the northern corner of Italy's Adriatic coastline. This tiny city-state, Venice, prospered in the burgeoning maritime trade of the western Mediterranean. By the beginning of the second millennium, its galleys were filled with the most profitable commodities of the era: slaves and grain from the Black Sea, spices from East Asia, incense transshipped from Alexandria and Cairo, and a host of other luxuries from the far corners of the globe.

Venice also found itself almost continuously at war with its more powerful neighbors and trading rivals, especially Genoa and the Ottoman Turks. In order to finance these conflicts, *la Serenissima*—the most serene republic—levied a curious kind of tax upon its wealthiest citizens, the *prestiti.*

Prestiti were bonds issued by the state that yielded 5 percent. The Venetian treasury forced the rich to buy these securities, and their purchase was onerous because the going rate of interest was higher, about 6 percent in peacetime, and as high as 15 to 20 percent in the teeth of a crisis, when the treasury was most likely to issue them.

Citizens paid the principal to a central treasury office, which then remitted periodic interest payments to their registered owners. The modern bond market was born when the treasury allowed owners to reregister these securities in someone else's name. Soon enough, what is now called a "secondary market" in prestiti arose, not only in Venice, but in other nations as well.

Figure 1.1 plots prestiti prices over the two-century span between A.D. 1300 and 1500, and what a saga this graph tells. For the first 75 years of this plot, Venice enjoyed relative tranquility, and prestiti prices remained lofty, trading as high as par (100 percent of face value). As late as 1375, they sold at 92.5 percent of face value.

Then, between A.D. 1377 and 1380, Venice fought a catastrophic war with Genoa. Initially, fiscal shock, not military defeat, damaged prestiti prices; the upcoming war expenditures forced the republic to suspend interest payments and issue a massive amount of new bonds. This depressed their prices as low as 19 percent of face value at the conflict's onset. Worse followed: In 1379, the Genoese penetrated the

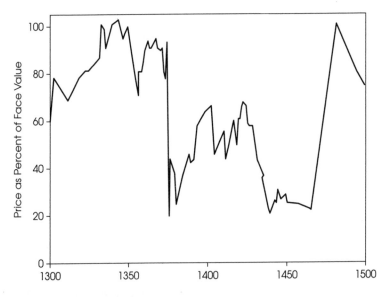

Figure 1.1 Price of Venetian Prestiti A.D. 1300–1500
Source Data: Sidney Homer and Richard Sylla, *A History of Interest Rates* (Hoboken, NJ: John Wiley & Sons, 2005), 99, 107.

lagoon, occupied Chioggia at its southern edge, used it to blockade la Serenissima, and nearly overran the island city. By 1380, when the city seemed about to capitulate, a daring last-ditch, counter-blockade of Chioggia by the Venetians broke the will of the Genoese and forced them to retreat.[4]

Thereafter, Venice's military fortunes improved, but continued high military expenses meant equally heavy issuance of prestiti, which kept their prices in the secondary market relatively low for nearly a century until the republic's debt was refinanced in 1482.

Once again, just what does all this medieval history have to do with today's markets? Everything and more, for the history of the prestiti demonstrates, at a relatively early point in financial history, the close relationship between risk and return. Venetians who purchased prestiti at high prices in the secondary market during the calmest years earned the lowest returns. Contrariwise, those who bought at low prices when things looked the bleakest reaped the largest rewards. The brave soul who purchased prestiti in 1377 at a price of 19 percent of face value in the secondary market collected not only 26.3 percent interest (5 percent divided by 0.19), but also a large dollop of subsequent capital appreciation as well. Of course, the risk that la Serenissima could have fallen to the Genoese, thus rendering the prestiti worthless, was substantial; hence the term *risk premium.*

This roller coaster ride aside, the price series of Venetian prestiti was a relatively happy one; la Serenissima continued to issue debt and pay interest on it for more than four centuries after its near-death experience in 1377–1380. Among developed nations, recovery from military and economic travail is the rule, and very high returns are usually made by those brave enough to invest when the sky is blackest.

Markets, however, do not always recover. Until World War I shut down the St. Petersburg exchange in 1914, the Russian stock and bond markets were among the world's most respected and active. They never reopened. During the twentieth century alone, military and political upheaval rendered not just St. Petersburg's bourse, but also many other once-vigorous securities markets, defunct, or at least moribund: Cairo, Bombay, Buenos Aires, and Shanghai, to name a few.

> For the past 200 years, things have always worked out well in the long run for the owners of U.S. stocks. History shows that it is entirely possible that our luck will run out one day.

Here is the central question for today's investor: Are we in Venice in 1377, or in St. Petersburg in 1914? In most aspects, today's financial markets resemble the former. They are indeed distressed, and for good reason. Although there is every probability that the world economy, and the securities markets along with it, will recover and provide courageous investors with high returns, as did prestiti in 1377, it is also possible that things will turn out worse than most predict. We just do not know for certain. Again, this is the very definition of a risk premium: the reward for bearing the risks of the unknown. Further, the greater the perceived risk, the greater the reward if things eventually turn out well.

The Incredible Shrinking Risk Premium

Eight years after lunch with my friend in the Chinese restaurant, the markets seem to have answered his question with a vengeance. Stock investors had indeed been stupid because they did not learn the lesson of just how risky even the seemingly safest assets can become, and even more critically, for accepting a low equity risk return premium for taking those risks.

In 2000, many finance professionals did indeed grasp the shrinking equity risk premium. Unfortunately, many of them, particularly my friend's brethren in the hedge fund world, made a fatal mistake: Since risk premiums were low, they reasoned, the only way to earn higher returns was by borrowing large amounts of capital to multiply—"leverage," in financial parlance—those paltry premiums. As so elegantly put by the dean of American financial writers, James Grant, in a slightly different context:

> Imagine a man at the top of a stepladder. He is up on his toes reaching for something. Call that something "yield." Call the stepladder "leverage." Now kick the ladder away. The man falls, pieces of debt crashing to the floor around him.[5]

Summary

- Throughout history, there have always been providers and consumers of capital; today it is no different.
- Also throughout history, that capital has taken two basic forms: loans (including bonds) and equity (partnership or stock). The latter has a lower legal standing than the former, and it is thus riskier and necessitates a higher long-term return to attract investors.
- During times of great social, political, and military turbulence, the prices of both stocks and bonds usually decline precipitously. Most often, this sets the stage for high future returns. Less frequently, however, the losses can be permanent and even total. Financial history demonstrates vividly the fact that just because this has not happened in the U.S. stock and bond markets *yet* is no guarantee that it might not occur in the future.

CHAPTER

2.

The Nature of the Beast

No balls, no blue chips.

—Old Wall Street adage

If you learn nothing else from this book, it should be that risk and return are inextricably intertwined. In almost every country where economists have studied securities returns, stocks have had higher returns than bonds.[1] Further, if you want those high stock returns, you are going to have to pay for them by bearing risk; this is a polite way of saying that in the course of earning those higher returns, your portfolio is going to lose a truckload of money from time to time. Conversely, if you desire perfect safety, then resign yourself to low returns. It really cannot be any other way.

Of Ravens and Returns

Let's start our journey through the land of risk and return by imagining a clear, crisp winter afternoon in the halcyon days of late 1998. You are out for a stroll, and as your thoughts turn to your financial health, your mood elevates. Your portfolio, which consists of a mix of judiciously picked stocks and bonds, has doubled in value during the roaring bull market of the past four years. While you have not done as well as your acquaintances, who are flush with dot-com options and aggressive tech funds, your modest portfolio has landed you squarely on the road to a comfortable retirement.

Suddenly, a winged creature lands on your shoulder. *Ah, you say to yourself optimistically, the bluebird of happiness!* Well, no; closer inspection reveals plumage of a darker hue. "Hello," it intones gravely, "I am the raven of capital market disaster."

This somber omen does not bring glad tidings. No, not at all: It warns you that within the next decade, there will be not one, but two historic market collapses. On each occasion, the broad market indexes will be cut approximately in half.

"Oh wise black bird," you implore, "please tell me when these two calamities will occur, so I may avoid grievous losses." You swear you see a smirk on its beak as it flies off silently.

Indeed, the raven got things exactly right; in the next 10 years you would suffer not one, but two of the five worst bear markets in the past century. Table 2.1 shines a bright light on these 10 years, showing returns for these two bear markets, plus the entire decade from 1999 to 2008, for some major classes of stocks and bonds.

The table illuminates the landscape of risk and return for the decade between 1999 and 2008. It displays a lot of data, so let's explore them column by column.

The first column simply lists the asset classes we are examining; the first 12 of them are the major foreign and domestic equity (that is, stock) classes, separated by three different criteria: location (United States, foreign developed nations, and foreign emerging-market nations), company size (large versus small), and whether the companies are of the "value" or "market" type. (The "market" designation means the broadest measure of stocks, which tend to be dominated by expensive glamorous companies, while "value" means the cheapest, least-liked companies that consequently

Table 2.1 Total Returns of Various Stock and Bond Asset Classes 1999–2008

Asset Class	Sept. 2000– Sept. 2002	Nov. 2007– Nov. 2008	Jan. 1999– Dec. 2008
U.S. Large Market Stocks	−44.92%	−40.48%	−13.77%
U.S. Large Value Stocks	−10.10%	−46.05%	+23.71%
U.S. Microcap Stocks	−17.58%	−45.18%	+86.63%
U.S. Small Value Stocks	+0.69%	−45.83%	+102.63%
Real Estate Investment Trusts	+26.28%	−54.77%	+107.14%
Intl. Large Market Stocks	−40.94%	−48.46%	+13.23%
Intl. Large Value Stocks	−25.87%	−54.12%	+59.02%
Intl. Small Market Stocks	−17.20%	−53.52%	+97.34%
Intl. Small Value Stocks	−5.68%	−52.42%	+148.23%
Emerging Markets Large Market Stocks	−32.61%	−56.13%	+147.67%
Emerging Markets Value Stocks	−26.79%	−62.01%	+251.38%
Emerging Markets Small Market Stocks	−27.59%	−62.91%	+196.43%
1–10-Year Treasury Bonds	+22.76%	+12.36%	+73.64%
1–10-Year Corporate Bonds	+22.80%	−5.45%	+60.41%

Source Data: Dimensional Fund Advisors, Barclays/Lehman Brothers.

sell for low prices.) Suffice it to say, this is the way that many finance professionals categorize stocks. The final two rows list different fixed-income (that is, bond) asset classes, generally perceived as being reasonably "safe."

The second column tabulates the return of these asset classes during the 2000–2002 bear market. The five years immediately preceding this, from 1995 to 1999, saw what was arguably the biggest stock bubble in the history of mankind. Investors went so gaga over the potential of the Internet that they regularly threw millions, and sometimes even billions, at 20-something entrepreneurs with only the vaguest of business models. Simply adding "dot com" at the end of a drywall company's name could double its stock price.

This madness also inflated the prices of the world's largest growth companies, which investors saw as the wired world's primary beneficiaries. Every other stock asset class languished. Real estate, represented by real estate investment trusts (REITs)? Bricks-and-mortar businesses were obsolete. Small Banking? Manufacturing? Retail Concerns? Toast in the New Economy.

As 2000 wore on to 2001 and 2002, the dot-com comets gradually burned through their cash and went broke, at first one by one, then en masse. The composite index of the over-the-counter (NASDAQ) market system, where the shares of nearly all of the new firms traded, fell by over three-quarters and the S&P 500 fell by nearly half.

But as seen in the second column, small stocks, value (that is, unglamorous) stocks, and REITs, which did not participate in the madness of the 1990s, held up very nicely, thank you, during the 2001–2002 bear market with REITs enjoying mid-double-digit positive returns.

The more recent bear market, shown in the third column, was an entirely different kind of grizzly. While the 2000–2001 decline was triggered when overextended, overenthusiastic tech companies ran out of cash, the current one began when overextended, overenthusiastic consumers ran out of credit. Furthermore, whereas the market froth of the 1990s confined itself mainly to tech stocks, the S&P 500, and its foreign equivalent, the Europe, Australia, and Far East (EAFE) index, by 2007 all stock asset classes had become overpriced as prices ran up dramatically in nearly every nation. Consequently, every stock asset class experienced similar severe declines. In 2000–2002, a few stock asset classes provided shelter from the bear—not so in 2007–2008.

The final column of Table 2.1 delivers the punch line: Even though our prescient bird correctly warned you about the two calamities that struck the markets between 1999 and 2008, it would not have helped over the whole decade. Fully eight of the 12 stock asset classes in Table 2.1 beat safe bonds during that period, as would have most reasonably diversified portfolios split among the 12. Had you heeded the raven's warning and avoided equities entirely over the next decade, you might have missed the salutary returns of a well-diversified portfolio. Worse, you would now be faced with the problem of when to buy back into stocks.

> Diversification among different kinds of stock asset classes works well over the years and decades, but often quite poorly over weeks and months.

The last column of Table 2.1 also gives the lie to something often heard today: Diversification does not do any good. True, on a day when the U.S. market is down 5 percent, the rest of the world will follow, usually with even larger losses, and in a year that the S&P 500 is down more than 40 percent, most other asset classes may do just as poorly, if not worse.

Investment wisdom, however, begins with the realization that long-term returns are the only ones that matter. Investors who can earn an 8 percent annualized return will multiply their wealth tenfold over the course of 30 years, and if they have half a brain, they will care little that many days, or even years, along the way their portfolios will suffer significant losses. If they are, in fact, anguished by the bad days and years, they can at least comfort themselves that the rewards of equity ownership are paid for in the universal currencies of financial risk: stomach acid and sleepless nights.

History versus Math

A familiarity with these sorts of short- and intermediate-term returns allows the prudent investor to understand the risks of stock ownership. Much has been made lately of "black swans": rare and supposedly unexpected events that roil society and the financial markets. In the world of finance, the only black swans are the history that investors have not read. Anyone familiar with the events of 1929–1932, which saw stocks fall by almost 90 percent in value (let alone what happened to the St. Petersburg exchange after 1914), would not have been dumbfounded by the recent market decline.[2]

The historical record, however, does not help as much with the most important exercise in the investment process: estimating future returns. Investors who cannot approach the expected-return problem rationally and systematically are better off putting half of their money under the mattress, then lighting the rest on fire and throwing it out the window. The good news is that estimating future returns is not that difficult.

In spite of this, many investors—even some accomplished academicians—do lean heavily on past returns to gauge future ones. This is a mistake. Perhaps you have seen a table that illustrates the nearly unimaginable wealth produced by long-term investments in large stocks and small stocks yielding annualized returns of nearly 10 percent and 12 percent per year, respectively, since the end of 1925. Well, you cannot have those returns—in fact, no individual in the history of the world ever has, or likely ever will. First, these returns are "theoretical"; that is, they incurred no brokers' commissions, bid-ask spreads (the difference between the buy and sell price of the securities), or taxes on capital gains and dividends. They assume away spendthrift heirs, who over the three or so generations covered by this period would surely have vaporized the assets. Last, and most importantly, we cannot go all the way back to the end of 1925, when U.S. stocks yielded 5 percent.

In fact, using historical returns to estimate future ones is an extremely dangerous exercise. It is even more dangerous to base financial planning decisions on the post-1925 database, a common zinger committed by many researchers and finance writers.

The two best examples of the pitfalls of an overreliance on historical returns arose in the early 1980s with bonds and in the late 1990s with stocks. The years following World War II were extraordinary in many respects. The most notable feature was the gradual acceleration of inflation, during which long-term bonds underwent a grinding bear market of historical proportions as interest rates rose along with the hyperinflation of the 1970s and 1980s. Inflation devastates long-term bonds, since their payments and final principal repayment are in nominal, or "current," dollars. If an investor buys a 30-year bond yielding an initial 5 percent coupon, and long-term interest rates subsequently increase to 10 percent, the value of that bond temporarily falls by nearly half.

During the 30 years between 1952 and 1981, long-term Treasury bonds returned just 2.33 percent on an annualized basis during a period in which inflation averaged 4.31 percent per year. Thus, on average, bond investors lost 2 percent of their purchasing power each year, even after reinvesting their coupons. Stocks, on the other hand, do relatively well during long periods of inflation, since companies can raise the prices of the goods and services they sell. During the same period, the S&P 500 returned 9.89 percent per year—more than 5 percent better than inflation.

In short, by 1981 the typical bond investor had been pulverized by the horrid past, or "realized" returns of bonds. Investors and finance journalists alike labeled these securities as "certificates of confiscation," frightening off an entire generation of bond buyers.

Yet, anyone who could add and subtract was presented with this calculus: On September 30, 1981, the government sold 20-year Treasury bonds yielding 15.78 percent interest, while during the previous five years inflation averaged "only" 10.11 percent. Further, by that point, the Federal Reserve, under the greatest of its chairmen, Paul Volcker, had dramatically tightened the money supply. By 1981, this had the desired effect of lowering the inflation rate; over the next five years, it fell to just 3.42 percent.

To summarize: By the beginning of 1982, bond investors had been hammered. However, a dispassionate look at bond interest yields and a reasonable estimate of future inflation suggested high returns ahead—at least 5 percent on a real basis. This hard-headed assessment was indeed borne out: Over the 20-year period beginning in 1982, the real return of the long Treasury bond was in fact 8.66 percent.

Another example of the dangers of an overemphasis on historical returns occurred in the late 1990s, as the prices of dot-com and tech stocks, along with large-cap growth stocks, soared into the stratosphere. Over the 74-year period between 1926 and 1999, the U.S. stock market provided investors an average return of 11.35 percent before inflation and 8.02 percent after inflation. Between 1995 and 1999, it clocked an astounding annualized 28.56 percent. Needless to say, the mood among equity investors was ebullient. In 1999, a popular mantra asserted that "Every penny you don't have invested in stocks will hurt you," while one of that year's personal finance bestsellers was entitled *Dow 36,000*. Sadly, this was not how things played out.[*]

How, then, can we reasonably assess future returns? First, let us admit the obvious: Unless we possess a crystal

---

[*]Political note: John McCain did not exactly inspire confidence in the financial community by appointing one of the book's authors as an economic advisor to his 2008 presidential campaign.

ball, we cannot do so with a great degree of accuracy. The best that we can do is to come up with what financial economists call an "expected return," one of the most important concepts in finance.

In order to understand this term, start at a roulette table in Monte Carlo, with 37 pockets (numbered 0 through 36; in America, there is a 38th double-zero pocket). The payoff on a winning dollar bet is 35 dollars, with a 1-in-37 chance of winning. On average, you will lose 5.3 cents of each dollar you bet ($\frac{35}{37}$ minus 1). This is the *expected return* of each roll, and also of the total amount you bet in any given period of time. Of course, on any given night, you may get lucky and make money or have a string of bad spins and lose more than 5.3 percent. This is the *realized return*. The expected return is thus simply the best guess of what your realized return will be on an average night.

Stocks and bonds work the same way as the roulette table, except that the expected payoff is almost always positive. If it were not positive, no one would invest. It is still roulette, but now the investor is the house. He will never know precisely what Lady Luck will dole out, but he can make a pretty good guess of the payout, particularly over future periods of at least two decades.

How do we do this? Begin with bonds. In early 2009, a 10-year Treasury note yielded just 2 percent. Since the government can print money if it has to in order to make good on its bonds, we were guaranteed to receive both interest payments and principal, so its expected return at that point was . . . 2 percent. (U.S. Treasury securities issued with a maturity of one year or less are called "bills"; from one to 10 years, "notes"; and over 10 years, "bonds." Notes and bonds yield an interest coupon every six months. Bills do not— rather, they are issued at a discount and redeemed at par; the difference is their "yield.")

Amazingly, in early 2009 the yield of 10-year bonds issued by the most solid American companies was about 7 percent. If all of these companies survived, then the expected return of a portfolio of such bonds over the next decade would also be 7 percent. Unfortunately, companies, including the most highly rated ones, do default and go bankrupt from time to time, so the actual return will be less than 7 percent after taking these failures into account.

Just how much less than 7 percent depends upon just how many of these companies fail. If more than 5 percent per year do, then investors would be better off owning the 10-year Treasury note. Most experts would estimate the long-term bankruptcy rate of such highly rated companies at no more than 1 percent per year, but in the present environment let's be overly conservative and call it 2 percent. In that case the expected return of high-grade U.S. corporate bonds would be 5 percent (the 7 percent interest coupon minus a 2 percent failure rate).

In Table 2.2, I have tabulated the range of possible outcomes. As already noted, only at a 5 percent annual default rate would investors be worse off than in Treasuries. What are the odds of one in 20 of the most solid American companies going bankrupt every year for a decade? In a worst-case scenario, this might happen over the next year or two, but a decade of such failures would be a cataclysm far worse than even the Great Depression.

Further imagine that the loss is an astounding 4 percent per year, and we eventually wind up with a 3 percent return. Even though we earned a 1 percent excess return over Treasuries, we would not be overjoyed, since that small margin would not be enough to compensate us for suffering from the risk—the stomach acid—of owning these securities. At a loss rate of 3 percent, corporate bonds are left with a 4 percent return, which is probably adequate to compensate us for the extra risk. Anything better than that is gravy.

Table 2.2 A Hypothetical Illustration of the Risk Premium of Corporate Bonds

Corporate Bond Yield	Loss (Bankruptcy/Default) Rate	Corp. Bond Return	T-Note Return	Corporate Bond Investor's State of Mind
7%	0%	7%	2%	Delirious with joy
7%	1%	6%	2%	Very happy
7%	2%	5%	2%	Happy
7%	3%	4%	2%	So-so: 2% risk premium (the 4% return minus the 2% T-note return) barely compensates for extra risk
7%	4%	3%	2%	Unhappy: 1% risk premium not worth extra risk
7%	5%	2%	2%	Very unhappy
7%	6%	1%	2%	Miserable
7%	7%	0%	2%	Shoots broker

Similarly, by the end of 2008 the bonds of companies of lesser financial strength, so called high-yield or "junk" bonds, yielded 22.5 percent, more than 20 percent higher than Treasuries. This daylight between the two, the junk-Treasury spread, was historically unprecedented. This meant that 20 percent of these companies would have had to go belly up *every year* in order to produce a lower return than Treasuries of similar maturity. After 10 years, this would leave just one in nine of them standing.

What are the odds of a failure rate this high? Very low, but not zero. Once again, junk bonds must offer a return premium over Treasuries to induce investors to buy these very risky securities. If that required premium is 5 percent, then in late 2008 up to 15 percent could fail each year in order to make their purchase worthwhile. (The foregoing example assumes that the investor owns a very large number of these bonds, or a mutual fund that invests in them. Obviously, if an investor owns a small number of bonds, an unlucky draw could mean the default of all inside of five years.)

To recapitulate: a reasonable estimate of the failure rate for the highly rated companies might be in the range of about 2 percent per year, leaving a 5 percent expected corporate bond return. Assuming that the long-term inflation rate is about 3 percent, this leaves an inflation-adjusted return of about 2 percent. In late 2008, for the junk-rated companies, the risk premium (the excess return over a 2 percent Treasury note) might have been as large as 10 percent per year, leaving an expected return of 12 percent on a nominal basis or 9 percent on an inflation-adjusted basis. The higher-than-Treasury returns for high-grade and junk bonds described above are the rewards the investor would have reaped for bearing the risk that the economy and, along with it, the default rate could actually be much worse than expected.

To repeat once more, the investor estimates the expected returns of bonds simply by starting with the interest coupon, then subtracting out the failure rate.

The relationship between risk and return is the single most important concept in this book. Recall that if 10-year corporate bonds yield 7 percent, but 5 percent of them per year fail, leaving us with the 2 percent Treasury return, this is not even-Steven. No, not even close: The corporate bonds churned our stomachs and kept us awake at night, whereas the T-note holders slept like babies. Corporate bondholders need to be paid a risk premium in return for their attendant insomnia and upset tummies. It follows, then, that the greater the risk, the higher the risk premium should be.

In fact, the single most reliable indicator of fraud is the promise of high return with low risk. Bernard Madoff's modus operandi involved only a slight variant on this theme: moderate returns with no risk. (Nor was this the only sign of fraud. All securities investments involve three operations: advising, brokerage, and custody. In any well-run, above-board investment operation, all three are conducted transparently. By contrast, Mr. Madoff conducted all three behind tightly locked doors.)

This point about risk and return is so critical that I am going to repeat it yet one more time: Investors cannot earn high returns without occasionally bearing great loss. If the investor desires safety, then he or she is doomed to receive low returns.

Mr. Gordon's Curious Equation

With stocks, the estimation of future expected returns is the same, except that we start with the dividend yield, then *add* the growth rate of those dividends.

Imagine that a company sells at $100 per share and pays a $3 dividend, or 3 percent of the share price. This $3 yield is money in the investor's pocket, to reinvest in the stock of this company or in any other financial asset, or to spend on groceries or BMWs.

Now suppose that the company grows its business, and thus its dividend, by 4 percent next year, from $3.00 to $3.12 per share. Since the market values the share price according to the 3 percent dividend and that dividend has gone up by 4 percent, in an ideal world the share price also goes up by 4 percent, to $104. Thus, we reap a 7 percent return—the 3 percent dividend plus the 4 percent increase in share price.

The same goes for the entire stock market. In early 2009, the U.S. market yielded a 3 percent dividend. How fast does that dividend grow? Financial historians happen to have very good long-term data on that question. Figure 2.1 plots the per-share dividends on the S&P 500 stock index since 1871. Notice how slowly they grew before about 1940, then rose more rapidly after that.

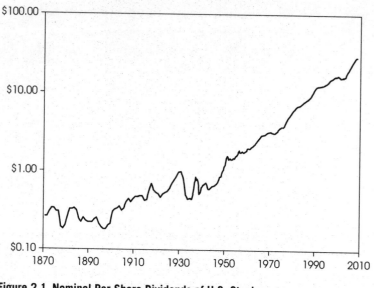

Figure 2.1 Nominal Per-Share Dividends of U.S. Stocks
Source Data: http://www.econ.yale.edu/~shiller/data/ie_data.xls.

The increase in growth rate after about 1940 is an illusion, as most of it resulted from inflation; the shallower slope before 1940 better represents the true growth rate. When the dividends in previous years are converted into 2008 dollars, a more accurate picture emerges, as shown in Figure 2.2: The inflation-adjusted dividends of the U.S. stock market increase at an agonizingly bumpy and slow 1.32 percent per year.

This illustrates another important rule of finance: *Always think in after-inflation, or "real" terms*; this avoids having to correct later for the effect of long-term inflation. In the end, focusing on real returns streamlines thinking and helps investors tune out the noise they will hear about how inflation "corrodes wealth."

The U.S. economy grows, on average, about 3 percent per year in real terms, and *total* corporate profits grow along with it at roughly the same 3 percent long-term real rate. Why do

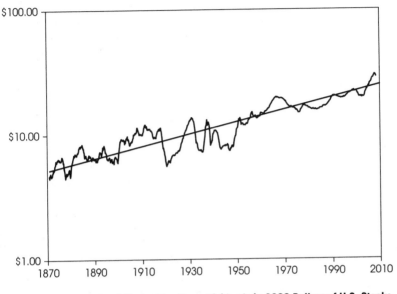

Figure 2.2 Inflation-Adjusted Per-Share Dividends in 2008 Dollars of U.S. Stocks
Source Data: http://www.econ.yale.edu/~shiller/data/ie_data.xls.

per-share dividends only grow at slightly more than a 1 percent rate, and not at the 3 percent rate of the overall economy? Because companies, like people, are born, live, and die, and new companies replace them. Investment bankers, bless their souls, sell the shares of these new companies at initial public offerings (IPOs), and these new shares dilute the existing pool by, on average, about 2 percent per year. So even though earnings grow by 3 percent per year, this 2 percent growth in the number of shares leaves only about 1 percent growth in *per-share* dividends. Yes, companies do buy back shares, but the 2 percent dilution takes these buybacks into consideration.[3]

Similarly, brokerage houses and mutual fund companies often tout the stocks of emerging-market nations, such as Brazil, Russia, India, and China (the so-called BRIC countries) because of their rapid economic growth. But beware: Share dilution, and often outright theft because of lax security

> Do not trust historical data—especially recent data—to estimate the future returns of stocks and bonds. Instead, rely on interest and dividend payouts and their growth/failure rates.

laws, vaporizes a lot of this growth by the time it reaches the per-share level. For example, China's economy has been growing at a blistering 9 percent real rate per year for more than two decades. Yet between 1993 and 2008 investors actually *lost* 3.3 percent per year in Chinese stocks, even with dividends reinvested. You read that right: Over this 16-year period, even before expenses, the investor in Chinese stocks lost 41.5 percent of value.[4] (The loss of 3.3 percent per year before inflation calculates out to a loss of 5.7 percent per year after inflation.)

Table 2.3 shows that the same is also true, to a lesser extent, for the smaller "tiger" nations of East Asia: Indonesia, Korea, Malaysia, Singapore, Taiwan, and Thailand, all of which had lower equity returns than the more slowly growing economy of the United States.

We can now finally estimate the real expected returns of equities. As we have already seen, in the case of the S&P

Table 2.3 Good Economies, Bad Stocks

Country	GDP Growth 1988–2008, Real, Annualized	Stock Market Returns 1988–2008, Nominal, Annualized
China	9.61%	−3.31%*
Indonesia	4.78%	8.16%
Korea	5.59%	4.87%
Malaysia	6.52%	6.48%
Singapore	6.67%	7.44%
Taiwan	5.39%	3.75%
Thailand	5.38%	4.41%
United States	2.77%	8.80%

* Stock returns, 1993–2008

Source Data: Morgan Stanley Capital Indexes, International Monetary Fund.

500, it is as easy as adding the approximately 2.5 percent current yield of this index to the 1.32 percent real dividend growth rate to get an expected real return of slightly less than 4 percent. This simple computation—simply adding together the dividend yield and growth rate—is known as the Gordon Equation, and it appears repeatedly throughout this book.

Expected Return = Dividend Yield + Dividend Growth Rate

It would be nice if dividends grew more smoothly, and even better if stocks maintained their price so as to yield a constant 2.5 percent dividend—that is, to sell at precisely 40 times the dividend amount. Unfortunately, markets do not cooperate that well. Over the course of the twentieth century, stocks have sold for as low as about seven times dividends (in 1932) and as high as 90 times (in 2000). However, over the long run these fluctuations average out, and the above calculation serves reasonably well.

Math Detail: The Discounted Dividend Model

Among early American economists, Irving Fisher towers above all the rest. Educated at Yale, where one of his advisors was the great physicist Willard Gibbs, he is best known for his infamous 1929 pronouncement, "Stock prices have reached what looks like a permanently high plateau."

Which is too bad, because among his many accomplishments was the basic mathematical method for evaluating the value of *any* investment or possession—be it financial, physical, artistic, or even spiritual. His essential insight was that the market price is but a pale imitation of the real deal: the pleasure or income stream an

(Continued)

(Continued)

asset delivers over time, discounted by the appropriate rate of interest for how far in the future each part of that income accrues.[5]

For an immediately consumed item such as a dinner, the answer is evident: You do not purchase that meal for $5, $25, or $125 unless it provides you with that amount of sustenance and enjoyment.

Next, suppose someone offers to sell you a meal listed on the menu at $25 for consumption 10 years hence. How much would you be willing to pay for it *right now,* and then have to wait a decade for it? Certainly much less than $25. Say you have decided that $5 sounds about right. Punch the numbers into a financial calculator and out pops an interest rate of 17.46 percent. That is your own personal "restaurant-meal interest rate." Or you could work the problem backward: pick 15 percent per year as the interest rate, and calculate that you will pay $6.18 for it now.

The key point is that a pleasure enjoyed today is almost always worth more than one enjoyed in the future. Fisher elegantly calls this the "impatience" for the item in question; it is synonymous with the rate of interest. Rare cases of negative item-specific rates of interest do exist. Perhaps you suspect that in 10 years the nation is likely to fall prey to war or famine. In that situation, you might very well be willing to pay a premium today for a meal 10 years hence. Probably the most common example of this involves fugitives from justice or persecution who purchase easily transportable jewelry, which they will likely have to sell at a loss, to pay for their escape and refuge. Once storage costs and insurance are taken into account, holding gold or jewels becomes even less attractive. However, money rates of interest are never negative, since you can always get at least a zero yield by packing your dough into a mattress.

People can have different impatience (or interest rates) for different items. Further, the rate for a given item depends on personal circumstances: A prosperous person is willing to spend much more today for a meal 10 years hence than a pauper. There are other intrinsic personal characteristics that determine impatience (or rate of interest); wastrels are by nature profligate and have high impatience, while thrifty people have low impatience.

Accordingly, the value of a stock or bond is its future stream of income, and in the case of a bond, its principal repayment at maturity, all discounted by the appropriate rate to the present.

Let's begin with a stock with a $3 dividend that is expected to grow at 6 percent per year. Let's further assume that the impatience of the investors, in the aggregate, for that money is 9 percent per year. Thus, the value of its future dividends, P, is:

$$\sum_{n=1}^{\infty} (\$3 \times 1.06^n) / (1.09)^n = P$$

Or, more generally,

$$\sum_{n=1}^{\infty} D(1 + g^n) / (1 + r)^n = P$$

where D = Last Year's Dividend, g = Dividend Growth Rate, r = Expected Return, and P = Price.

Applying a bit of integral calculus to the above equation, we come up with

$$P = D / (r - g)$$

which rearranges to

$$r = D/P + g$$

which is the Gordon Equation: Return = Dividend Yield + Growth.

Note that we have worked backward, using the price as the dependent variable and the return as an independent variable, then solving for the return. The reason for doing this is that when you are solving for the price, you may wish to assign a higher discount factor/return to a riskier asset.

What if the dividend yield changes over time? For example, between 1926 and 1999, the dividend on the S&P 500 decreased from 5 percent to 1.1 percent. This annualizes out to a price increase from this fall in dividend of 2.1 percent per year. By contrast a rise in dividend implies a fall in price.

(Continued)

(Continued)

Had someone known in 1926, for example, that over the next 73 years this would occur, and that dividends grew at a real rate of 1.3 percent per year, he could have computed that the real return over this period would be:

$$5\% + 1.3\% + 2.1\% = 8.4\%$$

Or, more generally, Expected Real Return = Yield + Real Growth Rate + Annualized Change in Valuation.

In actual fact, the real return of the S&P 500 over that period was 8.0 percent. Not too shabby.

This does provide a useful adjustment to the expected rate of return calculated by the Gordon Equation. Ten years ago, Vanguard Chairman John Bogle was fond of pointing out that such low dividend yields were highly likely to "mean revert"—that is, return to more historical levels in the range of 3 to 4 percent. This meant that expected real returns would be negative, a prescient analysis if there ever was one.

What now? Many observers feel that most asset classes are at least fairly valued, and that some, such as European stocks and REITs, are downright cheap. If these observers are correct and prices mean revert up, then returns should be even higher than calculated by the Gordon Equation.

To reiterate, the 4 percent expected return we have just calculated for stocks is a *real return*. This means that the value of the portfolio after taking inflation into account—its actual purchasing power—should, *on average*, double every 18 years.*

At the present time, many foreign equity markets yield around 5 percent. Even if their real per-share earnings do

---

*An excellent approximation of the doubling time of any investment can be obtained by using "the rule of 72," a mathematical rule of thumb dating to approximately the fifteenth century. In this case, divide 72 by the real rate of return: 72 / 4 = 18 years, which is very close to the actual doubling time at 4.00%, 17.67 years.

not grow at all, their real expected returns should be quite agreeable going forward: the 5 percent dividend.

Similarly, the shares of REITs corporations that own and manage shopping centers, apartment houses, and other commercial property, yielded about 10 percent in early 2009. U.S. law mandates that these companies distribute at least 90 percent of their profits as dividends to shareholders, which accounts for the very high dividend.

After paying out almost all of their profits to shareholders, REITs have very little capital left to purchase more properties or improve the ones they have. The gods of finance face them with an unpleasant choice: Either borrow capital in the form of bonds and bank loans, or not grow. The first path may produce growth but it is also highly risky, since being heavily indebted to banks and bondholders can leave them vulnerable in the event of a credit crisis, which is precisely what has happened to many of them in 2007 and 2008.

So, in early 2009, the best real REIT return that investors could reasonably hope for was 10 percent; if substantial numbers fail over the next several years, or even if they grow more slowly than in the past, this return could be lower. (As this is being written, REIT dividend payouts are falling rapidly; if, and how much, they recover will in large part determine their future returns.)

Let's summarize this chapter's lessons thus far:

- In the past, investors could expect only low returns when investing in safe assets; today, this rule applies with a vengeance to Treasury bills, which currently have a near-zero yield.
- Investors earn higher returns only by bearing risks—by seeking out risk premiums.
- To calculate the expected returns of bonds, start out with the coupon yield and subtract the annual rate of loss resulting from default and bankruptcy.

- Using the Gordon Equation—simply adding the dividend rate to the growth rate—investors can estimate the approximate size of future stock returns.

As already noted, the Gordon Equation often sends very different signals than do historical returns. For example, take a look at Table 2.1, which shows that over the past decade Treasury notes have actually had a higher return than corporate bonds. Yet, as just demonstrated, quite the opposite will likely be true going forward. Similarly, over the past decade, REITs, the S&P 500, and foreign large stocks have had low to negative returns, while the Gordon Equation suggests better days ahead.

On this point, financial history is clear: *Always favor expected returns calculated from the Gordon Equation over past returns, no matter how long of a period they cover.* This goes double whenever the markets are gripped by the euphoria of a bubble, as occurred in the late 1990s, or are in the throes of a panic, as happened in 2008–2009. If one of life's secrets is to be keep your head when all those around you are losing theirs, then the Gordon Equation is the collar that will keep it there.

We now have an even better case for the irrationality of equity investors that my friend and I pondered over at lunch in 2000. A decade ago, investors paid too much attention to historical returns and not enough to the Gordon Equation, which at the time suggested just a 2.4 percent real return for stocks (the 1.3 percent dividend growth rate plus the 1.1 percent dividend). They also forgot, or perhaps never learned, that history was rife, from the time of Venetian prestiti through the Crash of 1929 and the bond market of 1952–1981, with the potential for catastrophic loss in virtually all kinds of assets.

They also failed to match the risk with the return: The 2.4 percent expected real return calculated from the Gordon Equation in 2000 was nowhere near enough to compensate for the ulcers and nightmares that stocks are capable of generating. Something had to give, that something being a fall in equity prices large enough to restore dividend yields to levels high enough to compensate rational investors for bearing the very real risks of owning equity.

This has finally happened. The Gordon Equation currently suggests that there are better returns to be earned in both stocks and corporate bonds for the first time in more than a decade, perhaps in the range of 4 to 8 percent real returns for stocks of various kinds, and 2 percent real returns for bonds. Both of these, in my opinion, are high enough to compensate for the risks of owning them.

Home Sweet Home?

Let's pause for a moment and consider the item that makes up the lion's share of many, if not most, people's net assets: their home. How does this fit into an investment portfolio? Is it even an investment in the first place?

A house is most certainly *not* an investment, for one simple reason: You have to live somewhere, and you are either going to have to pay for it or rent it. Always remember, investment is the deferral of present consumption for future consumption, and if anything qualifies as present consumption, it is a residence. Further, if you pay for one in cash, then you are spending capital you could otherwise invest in something else.

Even if your home really is not an investment, the Gordon Equation supplies a way of thinking about the decision whether to buy or rent. Here is how it works. Just like a stock, a home or condominium's price should increase over time. How much? The best data on house prices suggest that, after taking inflation into account, the answer is slim to none.

These data focus on historical data from three nations. Real house prices in the United States did not rise at all between 1890 and 1990, while in Norway after 1819 real prices did rise, but only by about 1.3 percent per year. Amazingly, economists have even assembled a series of house prices along Amsterdam's tony Herengracht Canal going all the way back to the early seventeenth century. These show absolutely no increase in their after-inflation (real) prices for over almost four centuries—and in one of the world's best neighborhoods to boot.[6]

You can thus expect at best a 1 percent annual real increase in price. So far, so good. Next, just as with stocks, there is the dividend to consider: for a residence, the equivalent of the dividend is the so-called "imputed rental value" of the property. This arcane but important term refers to the fact that your home "pays you rent" every month. In other words, it makes little difference whether you rent a residence from someone else or you own it yourself. If you own the house outright, you are tying up a large amount of capital you could profitably invest elsewhere, and the imputed rent, or use of the house, is your reward for doing so. On the other hand, if you have the ability to pay for a house outright but choose instead to rent, your unspent capital can earn a return in other assets, such as stocks and bonds.

The opposite reasoning applies if you cannot afford to purchase the house outright, but instead require a mortgage. By choosing to rent instead of own, you substitute rent payments for mortgage payments. True, mortgage payments, at least early on, are largely deductible, but the advantage is more than offset by the catastrophic risk of default and repossession you take on with a mortgage.

Let's say you are considering purchasing a house costing $300,000 that might reasonably rent for $1,250 per month. This amounts to a 5 percent "imputed rental dividend" ($1,250 per month is $15,000 per year). Unfortunately, you have to subtract about 3 percent for taxes, insurance, and maintenance, leaving you with a 2 percent annual income stream.

> Home ownership is not an investment; it is exactly the opposite, a consumption item. After taking into consideration maintenance costs and taxes, you are often better off renting.

Thus, at most you will receive a 3 percent real return (1 percent real price increase plus the 2 percent net "dividend") on your home; if the current downturn in the housing prices perseveres, it could be much less.

A good rule of thumb is to never, ever pay more than 15 years fair rental value for any residence.* This computes out to a 6.7 percent (1/15th) gross rental dividend, or 3.7 percent after taxes, insurance, and maintenance, which is about what you might expect from a mixed portfolio of stocks and bonds. (Imputed rent does have one real advantage over the return from stocks and bonds, which is that it is tax-free.)

Until very recently, in many real estate markets, the own-to-rent ratio exceeded 20 years, which was a real warning that house prices had become excessive. In the coming years, home buyers may once again be able to make deals that pencil out in the above manner.

Finally, it should be obvious by now that a vacation home makes little financial sense unless you are leasing it out for most of the year. So if you must have a place in the mountains or on the beach, rent, do not buy.

---

*The figure I keep in mind when house shopping is 150: the number of months in 12.5 years. After hearing a realtor's spiel, I will ask, "So, what would this house reasonably rent for?" If the number seems right, multiply it by 150; this will give you an excellent idea of the home's fair market value, above which you are better off renting. I have found that this is one of the fastest ways known to man of darkening a realtor's face.

Adventures in Equity

Are there other risk premiums to be earned by intelligent, brave, and disciplined investors? There appear to be at least two more: the "value" and "small" factors. For many decades, students of finance have suspected that the stocks of value (that is, unglamorous) companies and small companies appeared to have higher returns than the overall market. In June 1992, two academicians at the University of Chicago, Kenneth French and Eugene Fama, finally confirmed these suspicions.[7]

In a *Journal of Finance* article, they conclusively demonstrated that premiums for both small companies and value companies exist. Professor French regularly updates these data, tabulated in Table 2.4, where he has divided up the U.S. stock market into large and small, and further into "growth," "mid," and "value," yielding six categories. "Small" and "large" are relatively self-explanatory, referring to whether the value of all the outstanding shares is above or below that of the typical publicly traded U.S. company: roughly $1 billion.

Professor French also divides up stocks into growth and value categories—shares that are respectively expensive or cheap relative to the assets the companies own. The former group tends to consist of glamorous, rapidly growing,

Table 2.4 Annualized Returns July 1926–December 2008

Asset Class	Annualized Return
Large Growth Stocks	9.02%
Small Growth Stocks	8.20%
Large Mid Stocks	9.75%
Small Mid Stocks	12.94%
Large Value Stocks	11.69%
Small Value Stocks	14.65%

Source Data: http://mba.tuck.dartmouth.edu/pages/faculty/ken.french/data_library.html.

"good" companies—think Wal-Mart, Amgen, Cisco, or, until recently at least, Starbucks—while the latter group tends to consist of doggy, poorly growing, "bad" companies—think Ford, Sears, or Caterpillar. The "mid" category contains those companies that fall in between growth and value.

First, note that, on average, the three small categories have had higher returns than the three large categories. This is not surprising; after all, small companies have more room to grow than large ones. Further, small stocks are certainly riskier than large ones, as well, since they have less diversified product lines and less access to capital and are more prone to failure.

What amazes and perplexes many investors, including professionals, is the fact that for both small and large stocks, the slowly growing, doggy value stocks have had higher returns than the rapidly growing, glamorous growth stocks.

How do value ("bad") companies tend to outperform growth ("good") companies in the stock exchange, when they manifestly do not in the consumer marketplace? Very simply, because they have to. Think about it: If Ford had the same expected return as Toyota, who in their right mind would buy Ford? *In order to attract buyers for its far riskier stock, Ford must offer investors a higher expected return than Toyota.* Although Ford may not survive, if it does, its shares will skyrocket. The company's stock somewhat resembles a dollar lottery ticket with a 1-in-10 probability of a $20 payoff. While you might not want to put a large amount of your net worth into a single company, the law of averages dictates that owning a large number of "lottery-ticket" companies should produce enough winners to make up for the majority of eventual deadsters.

Good companies most often are bad stocks, and bad companies, *as a group*, are good stocks.

Fama and French's work evoked a great deal of skepticism, even among investment professionals. Some critics complained that their data only covered U.S. stocks, so the two looked abroad and found that in 15 of 16 developed nations, and in 12 out of 16 developing nations studied, value stocks also had higher returns than growth stocks.

Others complained that their results were an artifact of the 1963–1990 period studied in their 1992 paper and could easily have occurred by chance. So they redid their study back to 1926 for the U.S. market, and found the same pattern of returns.

The third and final criticism of their work asserted that, although the small and value return premiums might indeed be present in the data, they could not be replicated in the real world because of transactional expenses. In the end, the real world of investing proved these critics wrong when one of Professor Fama's students, David Booth, helped found an investment company, Dimensional Fund Advisors (DFA), that closely follows the Fama-French methodology. Tables 2.5a–2.5c display the returns for 11 representative DFA mutual funds from near inception to the end of 2008.

Although these data only cover relatively brief periods, they fit the Fama-French pattern nicely, with small and value stocks having higher returns than growth stocks. Further, it is reassuring that these strategies were "battle tested," as

Table 2.5a Returns of Fama-French Portfolios in the Real World, as Executed by Dimensional Fund Advisors

Mutual Fund	Annualized Return Apr. 1993–Dec. 2008
U.S. Large (Market) Fund	6.37%
U.S. Large Value Fund	7.31%
U.S. Micro-Cap (Small) Fund	9.08%
U.S. Small Value Fund	10.03%

Source: Dimensional Fund Advisors.

Table 2.5b Foreign Developed Markets Stocks

Mutual Fund	Annualized Return Oct. 1996–Dec. 2008
Foreign Large (Market) Fund	3.04%
Foreign Large Value Fund	4.94%
Foreign Small Fund	3.75%
Foreign Small Value Fund	5.64%

Source: Dimensional Fund Advisors.

Table 2.5c Emerging Markets Stocks

Mutual Fund	Annualized Return May 1998–Dec. 2008
Emerging Markets (Large Market) Fund	6.94%
Emerging Markets Large Value Fund	11.38%
Emerging Markets Small Fund	9.33%

Source: Dimensional Fund Advisors.

two of the most severe bear markets in U.S. history occurred during the past decade.

Why, then, should not the investor own only small value stocks, the corner of the Fama-French world with the highest returns? There are several reasons. First and foremost, small value stocks have the highest returns precisely because they live in the riskiest corner of the equity universe. After all, they consist of the smallest and diciest companies.

Investors need to consider not only their financial portfolio, but also their "job portfolio"; that is, their human capital, or stream of employment income. To the extent that an investor might work for a small company or a value company, he or she does not want to own a lot of stock in such companies, since they will be subject to the same adverse factors as his or her employment in a downturn. Taking this concept to its logical extreme, one of the dumbest things any investor can do is to own stock in the company he or she investor works for, since he or she can lose both a job and portfolio simultaneously, as Enron employees found out to their chagrin in 2002.

Finally, small and value stocks can lag the market for long periods of time—the latter for up to 10 years, and the former for up to 20 years. If small and value stocks always beat the market, there would be no risk, so there would be no risk premium; the reward for owning small and value stocks derives in great part from this risk of relative underperformance.

It might be reasonable, then, to add 1 or 2 percent to the equity risk premiums for small and value stocks. Thus, U.S. small and value stocks have expected real returns of about 5 to 6 percent; for small value stocks, which have both risk factors, about 6 to 8 percent.

Let's summarize what we have concluded so far about expected returns for the major stock and bond classes going forward from early 2009:

Asset Class	Expected Real Return
T-Bills	–2%
Treasury Notes	–1%
Corporate Bonds	2%
Large Company Stocks—U.S.	4%
Large Company Stocks—Foreign	5%
REITs	6–7%
Small and Value Stocks	5–8%

So much for return. What about risk? In my previous finance books, I took great pains to illustrate its nature with descriptions of history's worst market crashes. This time the effort would be nearly superfluous; in 2009, investors need little convincing about the risks of stocks.

An easy way to measure the volatility, and thus the risk, of the stock market is simply to count the number of days the S&P 500 moved up or down more than 5 percent. During the last six months of 2008, it occurred 18 times;

during the 10 *years* previous to that, it happened only six times.

It gets worse. Among the world's major equity asset classes, the S&P 500 tends to be the best behaved. Between July and December 2008, both domestic large value stocks and small value stocks moved more than 5 percent 25 times, and international large-cap stocks did so 23 times.

Math Detail: Risk

Given a long enough series of returns and a working command of financial history, an investor can get a pretty good idea of just how risky an asset class is without resorting to higher or even lower math. That, of course, does not stop people from trying to measure it more precisely.

Financial economists usually start with standard deviation. For example, below are the monthly and annualized standard deviations (SDs) of monthly returns of several asset classes over the past 20 years. The monthly SD is simply calculated straight from the 240 monthly returns in the period, and the annualized value is obtained by multiplying that number by the square root of 12.

Standard Deviations of Monthly Returns of Various Asset
Classes 1989–2008

Index	Monthly Standard Deviation	Annualized Standard Deviation
S&P 500	4.19%	14.50%
CRSP 9–10 Index (Micro Caps)	5.97%	20.68%
EAFE (Large International Stocks)	4.89%	16.94%
Emerging Markets	7.01%	24.29%
20-Year Treasuries	2.70%	9.35%
5-Year Treasuries	1.33%	4.61%
30-Day T-bills	0.16%	0.57%

(Continued)

(Continued)

These numbers fit pretty well with the risks we adduced from the previous table, which showed their maximal short-term losses in the past decade.

The first objection raised by such numbers—usually by mathematically sophisticated but financially inexperienced observers—is that SD measures both positive and negative events, whereas investors concerned with risk do not care about events with positive SD.

This is baldly untrue. Almost all investments with high positive hemi-variance also have high negative hemi-variance, and SD thus gives you a second chance to catch a risky asset class. A classic example of this is afforded by the returns reported by Long-Term Capital Management (LCTM). Even before their operations jumped the tracks in 1998, their returns showed a very high SD, a clear warning of the risk embedded in their strategy. Put a different way, over the whole period of its existence, LTCM's positive hemi-variance occurred first, followed later by the negative hemi-variance; the SD of returns, even in the early good years, provided ample warning of the danger inherent in its strategy.

A more serious objection to SD is that security returns are not normally distributed and, in fact, demonstrate high skewness and kurtosis, the latter of which is extremely prominent. On October 19, 1987, the S&P 500 fell by 20.46 percent, and the Dow Jones Industrial Average by 22.61 percent—approximately -23 SD events for a one-day period—which has a probability of approximately 2×10^{-117}, about the same odds of your house suddenly undergoing spontaneous quantum decomposition then reassembling itself in a neighboring galaxy. Similarly, in 2008 the S&P 500 lost 37 percent, which is approximately a -3 SD event for a one-year period; this should occur only once every 741 years. Yet, this has actually happened three times in the past century alone: in 2008, in 1931 (-43.25 percent), and in 1937 (-35.02 percent).

As Eugene Fama puts it, "Life has a fat tail," while others like to talk about "black swans." A deep appreciation of risk involves not only statistically examining data, but also a working knowledge of history, particularly pertaining to the extinction of markets and of nations themselves; as I've said before, the more history you know, the fewer black swans you will sight.

Most of this is beside the point; no risk matters more to investors than that of running out of assets before they die, and this requires a long perspective. Because of the vicissitudes of history—financial, economic, political, and military—any statistical approach to this computation constitutes a frontal assault on common sense.

The most commonly used statistical tool is Monte Carlo analysis, where large numbers of normally distributed returns are computed versus a given pattern of withdrawal.

The results from Monte Carlo analysis are highly intuitive: The more assets one starts out with, the less one spends in retirement; the more one annuitizes, the higher the chance of success.

When all is said and done, I still know of no better risk analysis tool for retirees under the age of 70 than this simple narrative: At a 2 percent withdrawal rate, your nest egg will survive all but catastrophic institutional and military collapse; at 3 percent, you are probably safe; at 4 percent, you are taking real chances; and at 5 percent and beyond, you should consider annuitizing most, if not all, of your nest egg.

No asset class, however, has delivered the amount of stomach acid as have REITs, which moved up or down 5 percent in 45 of the 116 trading days in 2008's last half; more than 10 percent, 16 times; and more than 15 percent, three times (two of those, gains).[8]

The key point to remember about this volatility is that on none of those wild days was there *net* buying or selling of a single share of stock. Even at the height of the carnage, every share that was sold found a buyer, and on the days with the biggest price jumps, every share bought had to have been sold by someone else. On days of severe market declines, the talking heads will frequently remark that "sellers flooded the market," and that when the markets advance, "money came in off the sidelines." Again, no: For every dollar that came in off the sidelines from money market funds and checking accounts to buy stocks, a dollar of sellers' proceeds went right back to those sidelines.

Anyone uttering such nonsense should be pulled over by the finance police and forced to wear a bright red sign around their neck labeled "Rube." To reiterate, for every seller there is a buyer, and vice versa. All that changes is the *price* at which market transactions occur. When the news or sentiment about a stock improves, the price must rise to the point where eager buyers can induce the stock's holders to part with it. When news or sentiment about a given stock deteriorates, the price must fall to the point where potential buyers become convinced that they will be adequately compensated for the purchase.

Put yet another way, no matter how fabulous a company's prospects, a price exists above which its purchase will not yield an adequate return to its buyer. By the same token, no matter how dismal a company's prospects, a price exists below which an attractive expected return can be had, even if it is of the low-probability, lottery-ticket type.

Again, consider REITs. In all probability, their future returns will be high enough to compensate for the recent stomach-churning volatility; otherwise, no one would buy them. Contrariwise, there is no *certainty* that things will turn out well: no risk, no risk premium.

This sort of volatility and high risk premium last occurred in the Great Depression, and were I unduly masochistic, I might dwell on what happened in those years. Instead, I will simply show you a stock returns table for the worst bear market in U.S. history:

Asset Class	Return: September 1929 to May 1932
U.S. Large Growth	−81.4%
U.S. Large Value	−89.7%
U.S. Small Growth	−86.1%
U.S. Small Value	−88.4%

Source: http://mba.tuck.dartmouth.edu/pages/faculty/ken.french/data_library.html.

Throwing Dice with God

From the previous table, as well as the more recent market experience, it is obvious that few should own an all-stock portfolio. Two reasons mandate this. First, almost no investor, including this one, has the fortitude to lose half or more of his or her portfolio, let alone much more, as occurred in 1929–1932. It is one thing to look at a 50 percent loss in a table or a spreadsheet cell, and quite another to watch it happen to an actual portfolio. (Just as training for a crash in a flight simulator is a very different experience from the real thing.)

The second—and even more important—reason for the inadvisability of an all-stock portfolio is Pascal's Wager. The famous French philosopher Blaise Pascal defended his belief in God in the following manner: Suppose that God does not exist. The atheist "wins" and the believer "loses." If God does exist, the situation reverses.

The consequences of being wrong with each belief, however, differ starkly. If God does not exist, then all the devout believer has lost is the opportunity to fornicate, imbibe, and skip a lot of boring church services. But if God does exist, then the atheist roasts eternally in Hell. The rational person (or one who believes that the Almighty actually cares how he behaves and what he thinks), thus chooses to believe in Him.

In much the same way, rational investors today might reasonably believe that the economy will eventually recover and provide high stock returns going forward. If they were certain of this, then an all-equity portfolio would be the correct response to this assumption.

But investors cannot be sure; there is still the possibility of a 1929–1932 type collapse, or, as history teaches us, something even worse. If they split their money equally between stocks and high-quality bonds and they are wrong and equities do indeed collapse, then they are saved because their bonds will see them through well enough in a world where nearly everyone else is destitute. If they are right and stocks do very well, then all that they have lost is a somewhat higher standard of living because they did not go all-in.

> Always consider Pascal's Wager: What happens to my portfolio—and to my future—if my assumptions are wrong?

But suppose they go all-in with stocks and they are wrong. Then they are ruined. Wise investors hedge their bets with a large amount of bonds, since the consequences of being wrong with this choice are not nearly as dire as being wrong with an all-stock portfolio.

This gets to the heart of the investing process: The goal is not to maximize the chances of getting rich, but rather to simultaneously allow for a comfortable retirement and to minimize the odds of dying poor.

Consider what this means. The underlying subtext of most conventional financial wisdom is that the highest possible returns should be sought. A classic chestnut, for example, advises that the best way to accomplish this is with a portfolio consisting of a few carefully chosen stocks.

This is certainly true: If investors want to get filthy rich, then trying to find the next Microsoft and pouring all their money into it gives them the best shot. The problem is that since many, if not most, individual securities eventually go bankrupt, this also maximizes their chances of getting poor. (If you do not believe this, take a look at a stock page from a century ago and be amazed at how many of the companies listed went belly up.)

Gene Fama Looks for Angles and Finds None

I know what you are thinking: "Humbug on those low returns you've calculated! I can do better by carefully selecting the best-performing stocks myself, and if I cannot do that, I can find a mutual fund manager who can. Failing that, there are plenty of folks on TV, radio, and the Internet who seem to know where the market is headed. Surely I will be able to sell before the market crashes again."

Well, none of these strategies work. The reason why 90 percent of investors and fund managers cannot pick stocks is simple: Whenever you buy or sell a stock or bond, there is someone on the other side of that trade, and that someone most likely has a name like Goldman Sachs, PIMCO, or Warren Buffett.

There is even something worse than trading with Buffett, and that is trading with a top executive of the company whose stock you are buying or selling, and who likely knows more about its condition and prospects than even the smartest and best-informed security analyst. Trading individual stocks is like playing tennis against an invisible opponent; what you don't realize is that you are volleying with the Williams sisters.

Before we delve more deeply into the failure of individual investors and fund managers to beat the market, we need to become acquainted with someone whose name I have already mentioned many times: Eugene Fama. Growing up in a working-class Boston neighborhood in the postwar years, he attended Catholic school and then Tufts University, where he met Harry Ernst, a golf-loving economics professor, who was interested in the patterns of stock market prices and sold a newsletter based on his research.

Fama originally majored in French, but he soon got married and realized that better material prospects lay elsewhere. He switched to economics, and Ernst hired him as a research assistant. Fama's job was to search for profitable trading rules.

He found plenty, but in the jargon of economics, while they worked well ex post, they failed miserably ex ante.

These two quaint Latin phrases, that literally mean "after the event" and "before the event," respectively, are two of the most important ones in finance. It is pitifully easy to find strategies that worked beautifully ex post. Ex ante success (finding strategies that will work in the future), as Fama soon found out, turned out to be a much tougher nut. In fact, Fama was never able to find a strategy for Professor Ernst that produced excess returns going forward.* Why not?

First, let's start in the ex post world. Say you are looking at 10 characteristics of a stock that may have predicted future returns in the past. Right off the bat, 10 different strategies stand ready to be examined.

But it does not end there. Combining two of these 10 characteristics yields 45 possible strategies; and three characteristics produces 120.** Look at enough characteristics, and a nearly infinite number of possible strategies result. Purely by chance, a curious investor will find several that would have made him fabulously rich, *had he only known them in advance.* Statisticians call such 20/20 rearview vision "data mining." In a classic example of this phenomenon, one researcher found a near-perfect relationship between S&P 500 returns and the level of butter production in Bangladesh.[9] By random variation alone, some ex post strategies will fit stock returns closely; they will almost certainly fail ex ante.

To further illustrate this, imagine a stadium containing 10,000 people. All are asked to stand and flip a coin; those

---

*Peter L. Bernstein, *Capital Ideas: The Improbable Origins of Modern Wall Street* (New York: Free Press, 1993), 126–127. Technically, Ernst determined that Fama's strategies failed ex ante by "holding back" a portion of the statistical sample from Fama, then testing the strategies against this held-back data.

**$(10!/[8!2!]) = 45$; $(10!/[7!3!]) = 120$

flipping tails have to sit down, and those who remain standing flip again. The laws of probability tell us that, after 10 flips, about 10 flippers will remain upright. It is the same way with stock-picking strategies and active fund managers. Start with enough strategies or active managers, and purely by chance some will do well. Unfortunately, that tells you nothing about how well they will do in the future.

It slowly dawned on Fama that, in the long run, almost no one had the ability to predict stock market moves or to successfully pick stocks. Random variation alone mandated that some market-timing strategies would succeed and that some money managers might outperform others. Eventually, however, the law of averages catches up with all of them.

It followed that picking mutual fund managers and heeding the advice of market-timing strategists on the basis of prior performance were fool's errands, similar to the above coin-flipping exercise. Yes, someone always wins, but his chances on the next toss are still 50-50.

Fama would later get his doctorate from the University of Chicago, where he went on to a long and distinguished career. Among his many accomplishments was inventing the "efficient market hypothesis" (EMH) which states, more or less, that all known information about a security has already been factored into its price.* This has two implications for investors: First, stock picking is futile, to say nothing of expensive, and second, stock prices move only in response to *new* information—that is, surprises. Since surprises are by definition unexpected, stocks, and the stock market overall, move in a purely random pattern.

---

*There are actually three forms of the EMH: the strong form, which posits that all information, public and private, has already been impounded into the price; the semi-strong form, which posits that only public, but not private, information has been impounded into price; and the weak form, which posits only that past price action does not predict future price moves.

The EMH rocked the world of finance. For starters, it consigned an entire branch of investment strategy, so-called technical analysis, to the scrap heap. Chartists, or technical analysts, attempt to divine the future direction of stock prices from patterns of price movements, using visual images such as "double-bottoms" and "head-and-shoulders" patterns to signal bottoms and tops. The EMH suggests that the sole purpose of technical analysis is to make astrologers look good; Professor Fama suggests that perhaps it is better not to badmouth astrologers.*

Sandbagged by a Superstar

The implications of the EMH for the investor could not be clearer: Do not try to time the market, and do not try to pick stocks or fund managers.

The most spectacular example of luck masquerading as skill was the recent case of William Miller, skipper of the Legg Mason Value Trust. Between 1991 and 2005, he beat the S&P 500 *each and every year.* Such a performance could not have occurred by chance—it must only be the result of superhuman skill, right? Investors would have to be crazy not to invest with this genius, would they not?

It turned out that not investing with Mr. Miller was perfectly rational, after all. Between 2006 and 2008, he did so badly that he almost completely wiped out the previous 15 years' worth of outstanding performance. From the beginning of his tenure as manager in 1991 to the end of 2008, the fund managed to beat the S&P 500 by only a small margin: an 8.5 percent annualized return versus 7.9 percent for the index.

---

*There is some evidence of predictability in the price movements of individual stocks and the aggregate markets, but the effects are small and nearly impossible to profit from. These will be discussed in Chapter 6.

To get even those slightly-better-than-average returns, an investor would have had to have been one of his lucky first investors; in 1991, when Mr. Miller began managing the fund, it held only $750 million in assets. Anyone getting into the fund after 1993, at which point it still held only $900 million, would have been better off in an index fund.

However, by 1998, his performance began to be noticed, and it swelled fund assets to $8 billion; anyone purchasing shares at the end of that year and then holding on for the next 10 would have lagged the S&P by almost 4 percent per year.[10]

> When it comes to fund managers and market strategists, this year's hero usually turns into next year's zero.

By 2006, Mr. Miller had amassed more than $20 billion in assets, which he then took over the cliff, underperforming the battered S&P 500 by over 15 percent *per year*.

Were his story an isolated event, it would not be worth our attention. Alas, small investors incessantly chase returns the same way that dogs chase seagulls up and down the beach, but with far more serious results. The trajectory of Legg Mason Value Trust, with its a small number of early investors who earned initially high returns and triggered a stampede of gullible investors into the fund, who then got hammered when its performance returned not-so-gently to earth, gets repeated with a depressing regularity. In *The Four Pillars of Investing*, I related the nearly identical story of another superstar manager named Robert Sanborn—now long-forgotten—and I have no doubt that in 10 years, I will have my pick of carbon copies of Miller and Sanborn to relate.[11]

It is possible that Mr. Miller *was* skilled, but he increasingly labored under two handicaps, as do all fund managers.

First, his fund charged a 1.75 percent management fee, which came directly off the shareholders' bottom line. Second, all initially lucky and/or successful managers eventually sow the seeds of their own doom with so-called "asset bloat." In the halcyon years between 1995 and 2006, Miller attracted an increasing volume of assets. When a small investor buys or sells a few hundred shares of stock, he does not disturb its price—not so when Mr. Miller, or anyone else managing billions, tries to transact. Whenever he decided to buy, for example, a few million shares of a bank stock, he saw its price driven up long before he completed his buying. As soon as he was done, the price just as swiftly fell back to baseline. The opposite occurred when he sold.

Thus, his fund bought at higher prices, and sold at lower prices, than a smaller fund or an individual investor would. Finance professionals refer to the loss of long-term returns caused by the buying and selling of large institutional investors as "transactional costs," and in exceptional circumstances these costs can far exceed the fund's management fees.

Toward the end, the Legg Mason Value Trust was a financial bull in a china shop, smashing porcelain wherever it went. Worse, the overwhelming majority of Mr. Miller's investors came on board not long before the party ended disastrously.

More likely, Mr. Miller, his shareholders, and previous generations of performance-chasing investors, were, as the title of Nassim Nicholas Taleb's superb book on the role of chance in finance goes, fooled by randomness.[12] The search for outperforming money managers is called by some the Great Man Theory of Investing: identify the Great Man and, when he fails, search for the next Great Man.

What about Warren Buffett? No one questions that this legendary investor is skilled, but he has also suffered from the same asset bloat as did Mr. Miller; over the decade ending December 2008, his holding company, Berkshire Hathaway, has returned an annualized +3.27 percent. A respectable performance compared to the S&P 500's −1.38 percent, but remember, Mr. Buffett is a value investor, and while he beat the passively managed DFA Large Value Fund, which returned +2.15 percent, for the period, he lagged the DFA Small Value Fund, which returned +7.55 percent.

In truth, Mr. Buffett is not so much a money manager as a businessman; when he buys a company, he moves into a metaphorical corner office and helps manage it. Further, the story of Mr. Buffett's success is no secret; the market prices a "Buffett Premium" into Berkshire's shares: The Berkshire purchaser pays much more than a buck for each dollar in assets the company holds. The Sage of Omaha is getting on in years, and this premium will likely not long survive his passage from the scene.

The search for the Great Man burns even brighter in the newsletter business, whose publishers sell the notion that investors can indeed time the market. Hopefully, by now I have made you a little skeptical.

The most detailed study of this area comes from two finance academics, Campbell Harvey and John Graham, who looked at the performance of 236 strategies from 132 newsletters. Very few of them beat the market, and then only by a few percent, but several managed to lag it by between 10 percent and 40 percent per year, performance so miserable that it could not have happened by chance.[13] Harvey and Graham did identify a fleeting "hot hands" phenomenon. Newsletters with a few months of outperformance often continued it for a few more months, but these newsletters only managed to beat their peers; very few of these hot hands actually beat the market. Further, this effect was fleeting, shifting from newsletter to newsletter. In order to benefit from this temporary effect, an investor would have to subscribe to all 132 newsletters and determine for himself who had the hot hand that month.

The Harvey and Graham paper, however, does suggest an intriguing newsletter strategy: pick the *worst* newsletters, and do the opposite of what they recommend.

Jack Bogle Outfoxes the Suits

What to do about the inability of even the best managers to consistently beat the market, and the high costs of trying to? Before proceeding further, we need to become acquainted with another investing personality, John C. (Jack) Bogle.*

Like Gene Fama, Bogle was not born into the lap of luxury. After a shaky start that almost cost him his Princeton scholarship and college career, he graduated magna cum laude in 1951. It is not often that a senior college thesis changes an entire industry, but Bogle's—"The Economic Role of the Investment Company"—certainly did, providing a snapshot of the nascent mutual fund industry along with recommendations for its future. Soon enough, Bogle would use it to change the way people around the world invest.

After graduation, the Wellington Management Company hired him. Unfortunately, Bogle got caught up in the "go-go" era of the 1960s, the precursor to the 1990s tech bubble. Just as adding "dot-com" to the end of a company could juice its stock price in the 1990s, the go-go era saw the flotation of numerous dubious conglomerates and enterprises ending in "-tronics" that soon enough came crashing to earth.

---

*Full disclosure: Over the years, Jack has become a valued acquaintance. However, we have no business relationship, and neither do I have one with the company he founded, the Vanguard Group, aside from the fact that I am fond of its mutual funds. Further, it is no secret that his relations with Vanguard, which he no longer heads, have been rocky since he involuntarily stepped down as board chairman in 1999.

History often judges men by how they handle adversity, and the -tronics/conglomerates bust molded Bogle's character. First, like Fama, he became convinced of the costs and dangers of picking individual stocks. Second, he got fired. Bogle did not stand still for this; he had begun to think of Wellington as "his" company, and after a bruising boardroom battle, he convinced the directors of the Wellington *Fund* to declare their independence from the Wellington *Management*. The contest was in many ways unfair, since Bogle had at his disposal a secret weapon: a mastery of the Investment Company Act of 1940 garnered from his senior thesis research. When the smoke cleared, Bogle now had his own company, Vanguard, and his revolution was underway. Bogle began by creating a service corporation that actually ran the funds, and gave it the Vanguard name. Using the arcane provisions of the 1940 Act, Bogle assigned ownership of this service corporation to Vanguard's mutual funds, rather than to himself. *Since Vanguard's customers owned the funds, this meant, in effect, that they also owned the Vanguard service corporation.* Thus, all of Vanguard's "profits" flowed back to the fund shareholders themselves. Bogle had essentially turned the company into a nonprofit organization, run exclusively for the benefit of its customers. Although in the past many large insurance companies operated in this manner (think Minnesota Mutual), this structure is unique in the investment industry.

Next, Bogle applied the work done by Fama and others to the mutual fund business. He noted that the largest mutual funds charged about 1.5 percent in management fees. The efficient market hypothesis predicted that none of these funds could beat the market for very long individually and further, in the aggregate, active managers must of necessity lag the market by their expenses and fees, since *they were the market*. He then calculated by hand their average return and found that it was . . . 1.5 percent less than the market: "Voilà! Practice confirmed by theory," he noted. Vanguard would start the world's first index mutual fund. Initially derided by the investment industry as "Bogle's Folly," the Vanguard 500 Index Fund eventually became the world's largest mutual fund.[14]

Others followed in Bogle's footsteps. As already noted, David Booth, one of Fama's MBA students, with his mentor's blessing, founded Dimensional Fund Advisors (DFA) in 1982 (along with Rex Sinquefield, another University of Chicago MBA). The two dedicated themselves to the new passive style of investing. Next, the big fund companies, which at first did their best to ignore the new trend, eventually broke down and began to offer index funds as well. Finally, in the 1990s, a new type of investment vehicle, the exchange-traded fund (ETF), a kind of mutual fund that trades throughout the day just like an individual stock, and that almost exclusively uses the indexed approach, appeared on the scene.

Note that I have used two different terms to describe this new style of investing: "indexed" and "passively managed." These are not quite the same. The former means that a fund buys all of the stocks in an *index*, such as the S&P 500, whose composition is determined by a committee within Standard & Poor's Inc. Once each year, this committee replaces several of the 500 companies in the index; so too must any S&P 500 index fund. Another index, the Russell 2000, consists of the 1,001th to 3,000th largest companies ranked by total value of outstanding shares.

From the index fund perspective, this is a messy and somewhat expensive process, since funds following the S&P 500 must all scramble at the same time to sell the stocks exiting the index and buy the ones entering it. This mad rush incurs the kinds of transactional costs that plagued the unfortunate Mr. Miller.

The Russell 2000 index has an even more severe problem, since there is no mystery about the selection process, and speculators can easily predict which companies are going to be added and dropped on the changeover date. Just before this, these speculators will buy up the added companies and sell the deleted ones, bidding up and down their prices, respectively. This "front-running" dearly costs index funds tied to the Russell 2000.

By contrast, a "passively managed" fund essentially creates its own private index, specifically designed to keep turnover to a bare minimum. DFA uses this approach exclusively, then takes it one step further by purchasing stocks meeting its selection criteria that typically involve total market capitalization and the book value of the company's assets. After DFA has defined the list of stocks it can own, it proceeds to buy only those that can be transacted cheaply, thus preventing speculators from "stepping in front of" their purchases. In other words, DFA does not have to own all of the stocks fitting its criteria, only those that can be bought without incurring significant transactional costs.

Other fund companies solve the "indexing problem" by using less-popular indexes; Vanguard, after a royalties dispute with S&P, switched most of its index funds over to the Morgan Stanley Capital Indexes (MSCI) system, which relatively few other index funds use.

Fund companies can also employ a "total market" index that has almost no turnover. The most popular of these is the Wilshire 5000. This index, which originally contained the 5,000 largest U.S. companies, now encompasses 6,700 names and essentially owns the entire universe of domestic stocks. A company can only leave the index when it goes bankrupt and becomes worthless, is purchased, or absorbed into another company, none of which incur transactional costs.

In the long run, the advantages of the indexed and passive approaches over traditional active stock-picking are nearly insurmountable. Let's total up the average costs of active management for three different kinds of funds.

	Large Cap	Small Cap/Foreign	Emerging Markets
Expense Ratio	1.3%	1.6%	2.0%
Commissions	0.3%	0.5%	1.0%
Bid/Ask Spread	0.3%	1.0%	3.0%
Impact Costs	0.3%	1.0%	3.0%
Total	2.2%	4.1%	9.0%

The first row is the expense ratio that displays the sum of the management fee and other lesser administrative fees; the second, the commissions paid by the fund to its broker; the third, the spread between the buying and selling price paid by all investors when they trade; and the last, impact costs incurred by the managers of large funds, such as Mr. Miller's. The third and fourth rows together comprise the "transactional costs" of trading, discussed earlier in this chapter.

> Performance comes and goes, but for active mutual fund managers and their clients, expenses are forever, and few can surmount these hurdles in the long run.

An investor can easily find a fund's expense ratio in its annual report, prospectus, or online. Finding the commissions in the typical report requires a bit more digging. The last two expenses—the transactional costs—are not available to the general public.*

---

*Private vendors, such as Plexus Group, supply these data to their private clients.

In taxable accounts, active management incurs an additional penalty: High portfolio turnover realizes capital gains on which the shareholder must pay taxes. The typical large-cap fund distributes 5 to 10 percent of its value this way in an average year, and these distributions are currently taxed at 15 percent at the federal level, in addition to applicable state taxes. So investors should add in another 1 percent or so of performance tax drag on any equities held outside of a retirement account.

This plain arithmetic denies most of the mutual fund industry's very reason to exist. Given all of these disadvantages, how do actively managed funds survive at all?

Like the tobacco and gun industries, the mutual fund families become expert at rationalizing the inconvenient truth. Among the industry's many feeble rationalizations, eagerly swallowed by gullible investors, are the following:

- *Indexing did terribly last year.* It is occasionally true: Enough statistical noise suffuses the financial markets that in any one year, the bets made by some active managers will pay well enough to overcome the 2.2 percent of total expenses of the average large cap fund. Further, in those years when the S&P 500 is the worst-performing asset class, an S&P 500 index fund will not do well relative to its active peers that are free to own stocks in better-performing classes. For example, in 1977, 1978, and 1979, data from Morningstar Inc. showed that the Vanguard S&P 500 index fund beat only 15 percent, 25 percent, and 28 percent of domestic stock funds, respectively. Yet, over the long haul, index funds outstrip their peers. Over the past 15 years ending December 2008, the Vanguard Index 500 Fund beat 73 percent of active managers in its class, while its Total Stock Market Fund bested 68 percent.

- *Indexing works fine for large U.S. stocks, but the markets in small and foreign stocks are less efficient. In these areas, the investor needs the services of a stock picker.* The truth: Doubtful, but even if true, small cap and foreign stocks also have higher expenses. Over the past 10 years, the Vanguard Total International Fund beat 69 percent of active managers, while over the past 15 years the DFA U.S. Microcap and U.S. Small Value Funds beat 73 and 80 percent of their peers, respectively.

- *Active managers do better in down markets.* This is Easter Bunny territory, pure and simple. From January 1973 to September 1974, data from Lipper Inc. showed that while the average domestic stock fund lost 47.9 percent, the S&P 500 index lost 42.6 percent. From September to November of 1987, active funds did slightly better, with returns of –28.7 percent versus –29.5 percent for the index, but this thin margin is itself remarkable, since active funds generally hold 5 to 10 percent cash, and should have done much better. Finally, in 2008 the Vanguard 500 Index Fund beat 62 percent of the funds in Morningstar Inc.'s large blend category, amazing in light of the higher cash levels carried by the active funds.

- *An index fund dooms you to mediocrity.* This is true only if mediocrity is defined as beating 60 to 80 percent of the competition in the long run. Author and money manager Bill Schultheis likens the active-versus-index fund choice to a shell game in which the fund industry offers you 10 boxes, below which are hidden these payoffs:

$1,000	$2,000	$3,000	$4,000	$5,000
$6,000	$7,000	$8,000	$9,000	$10,000

On the other hand, an index fund pays a guaranteed $8,000. While it is certainly possible to beat that with the $9,000 or the $10,000 box, in most cases you are better off, and sometimes, far better off, by taking the $8,000 guaranteed payment.[15]

The shell-game analogy highlights the one legitimate criticism that can be leveled at an indexing strategy: It will never hit a home run. This gets to the essential nature of investing. As already alluded to, the name of the game is not to become rich as Croesus, but rather to avoid living out retirement in poverty. If you want to make a grab at the active-fund brass ring, be my guest; just be sure you like Alpo and Little Friskies.

Perhaps you are concerned that over some 10- and 15-year periods, up to one-third of funds appeared to have beaten their respective indexes and index funds. Do not be. First, the above data understate the index advantage. The Morningstar Inc. database suffers from so-called "survivorship bias," meaning that hundreds of poorly performing funds have disappeared from their fund universe, almost all of which would have underperformed the index funds. Second, the low returns of the past decade have given an advantage to the active funds, which hold a much higher percentage of cash. Soon enough, this will reverse. Third and most importantly, the saga of poor Mr. Miller shows that over periods as long as 15 years, luck still plays an enormous role in stock selection.

It Is Better to Be Lucky Than Smart

The interaction between luck and skill is one of the most misunderstood in finance. The simplest way to represent it is with a schematic that plots several dozen hypothetical

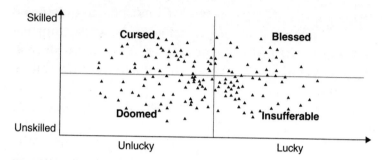

Figure 2.3 A Manager's Luck and Smarts
Adapted from Richard C. Grinold and Ronald N. Kahn, *Active Portfolio Management* (New York: McGraw-Hill, 1999), 479.

managers according to their allotments of these two qualities (see Figure 2.3).

Note how some managers have skill but no luck, and are thus "cursed," while others have luck but no skill, and are thus insufferable. I have intentionally drawn the "luck axis" much longer than the "skill axis," indicating that the former exerts much more influence than the latter. Did Mr. Miller and Mr. Sanborn begin in the "blessed" quadrant and then migrate to the "cursed" quadrant, or did they migrate from "insufferable" to "doomed"? The investor never knows.

It is impossible to overemphasize how much luck can overwhelm skill in stock selection, even over time horizons as long as one or two decades. Further, there is nothing magical about passive and indexed investing; any active manager who charges low fees, is highly diversified, and keeps stock turnover to a bare minimum should provide value to his or her investors.

Bond Funds: A Flatter Playing Field

Bond investing involves much less luck, and thus provides a much cleaner demonstration of the low-cost index/passive approach. While the range of possible outcomes with stock selection is enormous, one portfolio of Treasury, municipal, and high-grade corporate bonds performs pretty much the same as the next; here the advantage of low fees rapidly becomes insurmountable. Over the 10-year period ending December 2008, the Vanguard Short-, Intermediate-, and Long-Term Bond Index Funds beat 99, 96, and 92 percent, respectively, of their actively managed peers; and at 15 years, the Limited-, Intermediate-, and Long-Term Tax-Exempt Funds (which are not indexed, but rather purchase a broad, plain-vanilla spectrum of municipal bonds at rock-bottom expense) beat 92, 82, and 97 percent of theirs.

Stocks and bonds are just the ingredients; in the next chapter, we will learn how to chop, dice, mix, and stir-fry them into a portfolio. For now, let's summarize what we have learned.

Summary

- Risk and reward are flip sides of the same coin: Long-term high returns—the very best kind—do not come without occasional ferocious losses; perfect safety condemns the investor to low returns.
- On any given day, month, or year when stocks suffer severe losses, all equities will get whacked; only the bonds in your portfolio will retain their value. Over the long haul, however, the differences in the amount of wealth provided by different stock asset classes can vary enormously, and owning all of them helps minimize your chances of dying poor.
- The investor cannot learn enough about the history of stock and bond returns. These are primarily useful as a measure of *risk*; they are far less reliable as a predictor

of future returns. Never, ever, extrapolate past returns into the future, particularly when those past returns have recently been extraordinarily high or low.

- The wise investor estimates future returns for stocks with the Gordon Equation by adding the dividend yield to the dividend growth rate. For bonds, the investor estimates future returns by subtracting the expected failure rate from the coupon.

- During periods of extreme economic or political turbulence, risks will seem high. This will depress the prices of both stocks and risky bonds and thus raise their future returns. Stocks and risky bonds bought at such times generally earn the highest long-term returns; stocks and risky bonds bought in times of calm and optimism generally earn the lowest long-term returns.

- The stocks of small companies and value (unglamorous) companies generally have slightly higher returns than those of the overall market. This effect can be highly variable, however, and both small and value stocks can underperform for a decade or more.

- At the present time, the expected returns of all risky assets seem to be generous. The "expected return" is simply our best-informed guess; like a night at the casino, the range of actual outcomes is large.

- Investors should design their portfolios to minimize the chances of dying poor. A concentrated portfolio, while providing the best chances of making them very rich, simultaneously maximizes their chances of an impoverished old age.

- Investors should forget trying to pick stocks and mutual funds or to time the market. Although many individuals appear to be able to do this over short periods, they are almost always the beneficiaries of luck, not skill. The odds almost always catch up to them, as they did to poor Mr. Miller—and, to almost all of his shareholders. The best that investors can do is to maximize returns by minimizing expenses.

CHAPTER

The Nature of the Portfolio

Because we cannot predict the future, we diversify.
—Paul Samuelson[1]

Picture, if you can, a Japanese investor nearing retirement in December 1989. The Land of the Rising Sun is ascendant; appraisers value the land surrounding the Imperial Palace at more than all the real estate in California, and Japanese businessmen are gobbling up American companies and land like potato chips. Japanese manufacturers are devastating their European and American competitors with an endless supply of attractively priced cars and consumer goods. Within two decades, Toyota will sell as many vehicles *in the United States* as General Motors does.

Not surprisingly, Japanese equities have provided Japanese retirees with more than agreeable returns. In the preceding 20 years, $1 invested in the stocks trading in Tokyo grew to $57.23. Our hypothetical Japanese retiree should have looked forward to a retirement lush with family time, a Hawaiian condo, and all the material goods his heart could desire.

His story, unfortunately, does not end happily. Over the following 19 years, between 1990 and 2008, $1 invested in Japanese stocks fell in value to less than 60 cents, even with dividends reinvested. Since Japanese stocks were so ludicrously overvalued in 1989, there really were not many dividends anyway.

> Unless you diversify, you risk suffering the fate of post-1989 Japanese investors.

Consequently, his portfolio did not survive as long as he did. He withdrew what seemed a reasonable 5 percent of the initial value of his 1990 nest egg each year; by 2002, the money was all gone. Even more terrifying, he saw it coming. Just two years after retiring, the combination of market declines and withdrawals cut his portfolio in half.

Had he owned some bonds, he would have been in much better shape. And had he invested in the United States and European stock markets, he would have been sitting very pretty indeed.

As a U.S. investor, does this story make you feel complacent? It should not, because the same thing could easily happen to Americans retiring in 2008. Over the next two decades, American stocks could grossly underperform Japanese equities, as they did between 1970 and 1989. More likely, some other foreign or domestic stock or bond asset class will outperform both. Or maybe U.S. stocks will again top the list. We simply do not know.

Why not avoid risk altogether and sock away all your assets in Treasury bills or insured certificates of deposit (CDs)? For the typical retiree, this is not an option. According to the Social Security Agency, the average 65-year-old man and woman will live to be 81.67 and 84.50, respectively. If they make it to those ages, then they will each have additional life expectancies of seven more years. Thus, the odds are good that one of them will survive to 90, and, because of improvements in lifestyle and medical care, one of them could easily make it to 95.[2]

Treasury bills currently have a near-zero yield, and historically inflation has averaged about 3 percent. Accordingly, retirees who spend 5 percent of their portfolios each year and lose 3 percent more to inflation will see the real value of their savings deplete at roughly 8 percent per year, and they will run out of money in about 12.5 years. This, mind you, is a best-case scenario, since it does not take the ravages of unexpected higher inflation or an expensive illness into account.

For young savers, investing only in "safe" assets is even more of a disaster, since their retirement nest eggs will not grow adequately in the first place. If we learned anything from the first chapter, it is that investors cannot earn decent returns without taking risks. In the current environment, risks seem very high, and because investors need to be compensated for bearing these risks, returns going forward should of necessity also be high. Further, the surest way to obtain those high returns will be to diversify widely among risky assets.

Four Essential Preliminaries

Before diving into the most important issue faced by any investor—the asset allocation decision—you will need to understand four things: save as much as you can, make sure you have enough liquid taxable assets for emergencies, diversify widely, and do so with passive or index funds.

- If you cannot save, do not waste your time on this book. Always remember the textbook definition of investment: the deferral of current consumption for future consumption. If you cannot defer current consumption, you will die poor, even if you are possessed of Warren-Buffett-like investment acumen.

Save as much as you can, and do not stop saving until you die. Lately, some financial economists have embraced the concept of "consumption smoothing," which means maintaining an even standard of living throughout life, and they caution against "oversaving" (deferring too much consumption during your prime years). Always remember Pascal's Wager: the imperative to avoid the worst-case scenario. The consequences of oversaving pale next to those of undersaving; today, all over America, tens of millions are thankful that they have saved "too much," and hundreds of millions rue that they saved too little.

- In the same vein, before you begin building your long-range portfolio, put away enough savings to sustain you for at least six months in the event of job loss or serious illness. This should be in a taxable account, so as to avoid the severe penalties of withdrawing funds from an IRA or 401(k) before reaching the minimum retirement age of 59½. (Retirees can make penalty-free withdrawals before age 59½ under the IRS's "substantially equal payments," or "72(t)" rule, but beware: the costs of not precisely following IRS regulations in such circumstances are high.)

This book deals only with the longest-range savings decisions, such as for retirement, prolonged philanthropic giving, children's and grandchildren's trust funds, and perhaps saving for college more than 15 years hence. Further, this book most definitely does not deal in detail with money needed in less than five years, such as saving for a house down payment. Here, the play book is very thin: Keep such funds in the safest, short-duration vehicles as possible, such as high-grade, short-term bonds and CDs. If you decide to buy bonds or a bond fund, make sure the average maturity is less than the time horizon of the savings. The last thing you want to do is to put your house down payment money into equities, that recent experience shows can fall in value by half within 12 months.

- Diversify as widely as you can. While it is possible for you to construct a "do-it-yourself" portfolio of stocks and bonds, you would be foolish to do so.

- Just like people, most companies, given enough time, die. Paradoxically, over a 10-year period, about two-thirds of stocks underperform the market; most market return comes from relatively few companies that succeed mightily, such as 115-year-old General Electric.[3] Mergers and spin-offs also contribute, as occurred with the breakups of AT&T and Standard Oil in the last century.

  You may have heard that you can get adequate diversification by owning 15 or 30 stocks. In a narrow statistical sense, this is true; a portfolio of a relatively small number of stocks is not much more volatile than the overall market on a daily basis. This fact misses a much larger point: Small portfolios, even with their low volatility, are more likely to send you to the poorhouse. Researcher Ron Surz constructed 1,000 random portfolios each containing 15 stocks, and then followed their performance for 30 years. The "lucky" portfolios at the 95th percentile or better returned 2.5 times the end wealth of the market, but the "unlucky" ones at the fifth percentile returned only 40 percent of the final wealth of the market.[4]

- Yes, picking a small number of stocks increases your chances of getting rich, but as we just learned, it also increases your chances of getting poor. By buying and holding the entire market through a passively managed or indexed mutual fund, you guarantee that you will own all of the winning companies and thus get all of the market return. True, you will own all of the losers as well, but that is not as important; the most that can vanish with any one stock is 100 percent of its purchase value, whereas the winners can easily make 1,000 percent, and exceptionally 10,000 percent, inside of a decade or two. Miss just one or two of these winning stocks, and your entire portfolio will suffer. For example, a Wilshire 5000-type "total stock market" fund essentially owns the stocks of all U.S. publicly traded companies, and it is difficult to get more diversified than that. Such indexed portfolios can be bought from the major mutual fund companies for as little as 0.07 percent in annual fees, which is much less than you would pay to buy and hold a large list of stocks yourself.

The Asset Allocation Two-Step

With these preliminaries out of the way, we can finally begin to discuss the asset allocation process: how to combine the asset classes we covered in Chapter 1 into real-world investment portfolios. The good news is it is really not that hard: The investor only makes two important decisions:

1. The overall allocations to stocks and bonds.
2. The allocation among stock asset classes.

We'll approach the first decision, the overall stock/bond split, with a parable from one of investment management's great sages, Charley Ellis:

> **Question**: If you had your own choice, which would you prefer?
> Choice A: Stocks go *up* by quite a lot—and *stay up* for many years.
> Choice B: Stocks go *down* by quite a lot—and *stay down* for many years.[5]

This is a trick question, of course. While most investors would pick choice A, Ellis points out that the long-term investor should clearly prefer choice B.

In order to understand why, let's take another look at the Gordon Equation for U.S. stocks in 2009. The expected return is currently a 2.5 percent yield plus the 1.32 percent historical dividend growth rate. Thus, the ongoing dividend stream, not its expected growth, provides the lion's share of return. Again, Ellis:

> Just as we buy cows for their milk and hens for their eggs, we buy stocks for their current and future dividends. If you ran a dairy, wouldn't you prefer to have cow prices low when you were buying, so you could get more gallons of milk for your investment in cows?[6]

Or, as the old Wall Street ditty goes, "Milk from the cows, eggs from the hens. A stock, by God, for its dividends." The longer the time horizon, the more powerful this analysis becomes. A 25-year-old who is actively saving for retirement should get down on his knees and pray for a decades-long, brutal bear market so that he can accumulate stocks cheaply.

The rosiest scenario for the young investor is a long, brutal bear market. For the retiree, it most definitely is not.

Things look a little different for the older person, however, as we already saw with our unfortunate Japanese investor. The bear market is no friend of the retiree, who is spending down his or her savings.

As a general rule, then, the conventional wisdom that young people should invest more aggressively than older individuals is quite correct. The reason usually given for this is that stocks somehow become safer over longer periods. But as the history of the markets in St. Petersburg, Cairo, New Delhi, and Buenos Aires during the early twentieth century shows, this is most definitely *not* the case.

Rather, younger investors should own a higher portion of stocks because they have the ability to apply their regular savings to the markets at depressed prices. More precisely, young investors possess more "human capital" than financial capital; that is, their total future earnings dwarf their savings and investments. From a financial perspective, human capital looks like a bond whose coupons escalate with inflation.

Since young workers can be said to be the owners of a huge bond-like asset, their human capital, they can hold most, if not all, of their investment capital as stocks. Or so the theory goes.

A retired person, by contrast, has no human capital left (unless he or she wishes to count his or her Social Security payments), and thus cannot buy more equity if stock prices fall, so it would be unwise for him or her to invest too aggressively.

The vast majority of investors fall somewhere in between these two extremes, so that typical middle-aged persons, as a first approximation, might want to divide their financial assets evenly between stocks and bonds. Thus, age is the first factor in determining the overall stock/bond allocation.

Investor risk tolerance is the second. Once again, the recent bear market has made my job immeasurably easier in this regard. In the course of writing two finance books between 1995 and 2001, I had to expend considerable effort performing the following task, so admirably described by journalist Fred Schwed nearly a century ago:

> There are certain things that cannot be adequately explained to a virgin either by words or pictures. Nor can any description that I might offer here even

approximate what it feels like to lose a real chunk of money that you used to own.[7]

By 2009, nearly all investors had lost their virginity. All can now respond accurately, without benefit of words or pictures, to the question, "How well do you tolerate financial risk?" More to the point, over the past few years, did the investor (a) sell, (b) hold steady, (c) buy more, or (d) buy more and hope for even further declines so as to continue the process? The answers to this risk-tolerance question are then, respectively, "low," "moderate," "high," and "very high." The exact same answers could also be given to the question, "How disciplined are you?" No one said this was easy.

The most common rule of thumb dictates a bond allocation equal to the investor's age. Thus, a 20-year-old should hold an 80/20 stock/bond portfolio, whereas a 70-year-old should hold a 30/70 portfolio. The investor could perhaps modify his or her allocation according to risk tolerance in the following manner:

Risk Tolerance	Adjustment to the Bond Allocation = Age Rule	Example: Stock/Bond for a 50-Year-Old
Very High	+20%	70/30%
High	+10%	60/40%
Moderate	0%	50/50%
Low	−10%	40/60%
Very Low	−20%	30/70%

Thus, combining the bond-allocation-equals-age rule with this risk-tolerance assessment, a 50-year-old with very high risk tolerance and a 30-year-old with moderate risk tolerance might both have the same 70/30 stock/bond allocation. A 90-year-old with average risk tolerance and a

70-year-old with very low risk tolerance both might want to own a 10/90 stock/bond portfolio.

This scheme provides just a starting point. An extremely wealthy 80-year-old who lives off of less than 1 percent of her portfolio might reasonably invest much more aggressively than most folks her age, since it is very unlikely she will run out of money no matter how high her equity exposure is. In reality, her portfolio belongs more to her heirs and philanthropic endeavors than to herself.

On the other hand, a 70-year-old whose living expenses consume 7 percent of his portfolio each year would be well advised to reduce his expenditures, and theoretically spend most of his nest egg on a fixed annuity—contracts sold by insurance companies that guarantee lifelong income purchased with an up-front fixed sum. This would assure him a decent monthly payment should he live too long. Unfortunately, we will find in Chapter 5 that although fixed annuities theoretically offer "longevity insurance," the ongoing problems of their sellers, the insurance companies, render their current purchase problematic.

> The most important asset allocation decision is the overall stock/bond mix; start with the age = bond allocation rule of thumb.

Further, young people tend to overestimate their risk tolerance; risk is an acquired taste. Recall Mr. Schwed's bon mot: It is one thing for investors to look at a spreadsheet when they are 25 and decide that they can tolerate an 80/20 portfolio that might, under extraordinary circumstances, lose 40 percent of its value. It is something else entirely to live through such misfortune with equanimity.

Older individuals, on the other hand, have survived bear markets; they know market declines usually end. Not infrequently, they lament having missed buying low when they were younger and resolve that next time, they will take that opportunity.

A classic case of such elder wisdom played out in the late 1970s and early 1980s, when *BusinessWeek* proclaimed "The Death of Equities" in a famous 1979 cover story. For more than a decade before the article's publication, stocks had languished with low, single-digit returns that lagged the high rate of inflation. Nearly everyone had lost faith in stocks . . . except the elderly:

> Between 1970 and 1975, the number of investors declined in every age group but one: individuals 65 and older. While the number of investors under 65 dropped by about 25%, the number of investors over 65 jumped by more than 30%. Only the elderly who have not understood the changes in the nation's financial markets, or who are unable to adjust to them, are sticking with stocks.

The article went on to quote a young corporate executive:

> Have you been to an American stockholders' meeting lately? They're all old fogies. The stock market is just not where the action's at.[8]

The joke, of course, was on the young executive and on *BusinessWeek*, which never lived down the "The Death of Equities." This infamous article heralded the beginning of one of the longest and most powerful bull markets in U.S. history. The elderly, it turned out, knew the score after all. Unlike the young, they recognized the pessimism and low equity prices from their Depression-era youth and understood fully what they meant—high returns ahead.

Thus one of the bittersweet paradoxes of investing: Long and deep market declines are wasted on the young. Although they should be heavily invested in equities, they are usually too frightened by their first encounter with the bear to buy. Equally, bear markets are wasted on the old, whose lack of human capital and the fact that they are drawing down their portfolios   dictate a low equity exposure. Only with effort and discipline can young and middle-aged persons acquire a command of market history, morph into "*BusinessWeek* Old Fogies," and take advantage of such opportunities before their time.

> The best time to buy stocks is often when the economic clouds are the blackest, and the worst times to buy are when the sky is the bluest.

As you gain experience, you will develop a better sense of your actual risk tolerance. One useful paradigm for assessing an appropriate stock/bond mix involves what I call the "equipoise point." Here is how it works: During a bull market you will derive pleasure from your stock gains and will regret that you were not more heavily invested; your equipoise point is that allocation at which this pleasure and regret exactly counterbalance each other. Similarly, during substantial market declines, the equipoise point is that allocation where the pain of loss in stocks exactly counterbalances the warm fuzzy feeling provided by your bonds and the capacity they provide to buy more stocks at low prices.

Once you have decided on your stock/bond split, your next big task is to allocate the stock assets. As a very rough first approximation, a belief in market efficiency should make this process simple: buy and hold the entire market basket of the world's stocks. The Financial Times Stock

Exchange indexes (FTSE—pronounced "footsie") is a joint venture of the *Financial Times* newspaper and the London Stock Exchange that maintains a "world index" which does just that. Figure 3.1 shows how it allocated its holdings on December 31, 2008.

The signal characteristic that defines this index is that it is "market cap-weighted." This term means that an index, and thus any index fund based on it, holds a given company according to the dollar value of all shares. For example, on 12/31/08, the index's largest single component, ExxonMobil, accounted for 1.9 percent of the fund, because the total value of this company's shares constituted 1.9 percent of the value of all of the world's stocks. One of its smaller components, the Czech oil company Unipetrol a.s., constituted only 0.001 percent of the index, again, because

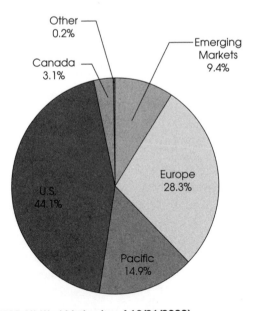

Figure 3.1 FTSE All-World Index (as of 12/31/2008)

its market cap accounted for 0.001 percent of the value of the world's stocks.*

The beauty of cap-weighting is that it is "fire and forget"; no matter what the stock price does, the fund manager does not have to buy or sell. If the company's stock quadruples relative to the rest of the index, so does its share of the index and of any index fund that mimics it. The same happens if its stock price falls—so will its market cap fall, and so will its representation in the index. Remember, buying and selling costs money, and the less of it you do, the better. For a mutual fund, because of the high transactional costs of trading large share volumes, this goes double.

You can purchase this index in a single vehicle from Vanguard: the Total World Stock Index Fund. I do not recommend it, however. The 44/56 United States/foreign split of this fund, and of its underlying index, is too foreign-heavy for my taste for three reasons. First, unless you are living abroad, you are going to be spending mainly dollars in retirement, and the foreign stocks will expose you to the risk of depreciation of the euro, yen, pound, and other foreign currencies. Second, not only are foreign stocks riskier than U.S. stocks, they are also more expensive to own. It costs more to transact abroad, and many foreign governments tax stock dividends; although you can recover this cost in a taxable account through the foreign tax credit on your U.S. tax return, you cannot do so in a retirement account. Last, the fund's fees are higher than they need to be, uncharacteristic of a Vanguard offering. At a 0.50 percent expense ratio plus a 0.25 percent purchase fee, an investor can

---

*In practice, the FTSE World Index, and the Vanguard Total World Stock Index Fund that tracks it, weights its holdings according to a slightly different metric: the dollar value of shares outstanding available for public trading, the so-called "free float."

separately buy its components—the United States and international stock markets—much more cheaply.

Math Detail: Mean-Variance Analysis

In a 1952 article in the *Journal of Finance,* Harry Markowitz rocked the investment world with a revolutionary notion: Investors cared as much about risk as return.[9] His key insight about the relationship between the two was that at any given level of risk, there was a portfolio that delivered the optimal return, and that at any given level of return, there was a portfolio that exposed the investor to a minimum level of risk.

I have represented this paradigm graphically below, which demonstrates a "cloud" of portfolios in mean-variance space.

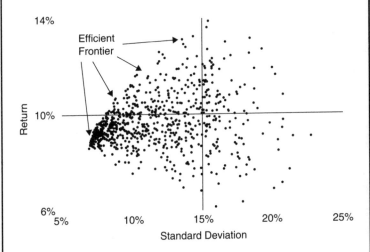

First, focus on the vertical line at 15 percent SD. Note that there are many portfolios that lie on or near it; obviously, you want that portfolio nearest the top of this line, earning the highest return for that degree of risk. Similarly, note all the portfolios at or near the horizontal line at 10 percent; just as obviously, you want to

(Continued)

(Continued)

be all the way to the right of the cloud, earning that return with the lowest degree of risk.

The upper left border of that cloud, which forms a reasonably well-defined convex border, is where you wish to find yourself: the so-called efficient frontier. Markowitz's genius was in deriving an algorithm that solves for all the portfolios that lie along the efficient frontier. Its inputs are the returns and SDs of all of the possible assets, and the correlation grid among them.

Although Markowitz described his method—called *mean variance optimization* (MVO)—in 1952, the computing power required for typical portfolios did not come along until the personal computer revolution of the 1980s. At this point financial analysts began plugging historical data willy-nilly into commercial MVO software.

The results were disastrous. Since MVO tends to select the assets with the highest inputted returns, it was heavy in foreign— particularly Japanese—stocks, precisely the worst asset classes going forward. Slowly, it dawned on financial analysts that, because of the long-run tendency of asset class returns to mean revert, MVO functioned in reality as an "error maximizer," overweighting/under-weighting assets that tended to have lower/higher future returns.

In my opinion, MVO is primarily useful as a teaching tool, but investors should avoid it when it comes time to design real-world portfolios.

With Luck, Zigs, and Zags

Let's now turn to the benefits of diversification, and just how to mix together different kinds of assets—so-called "portfolio theory." This can get highly technical, and, for those who are interested, I have provided an introduction to the subject in the Math Detail section.

The non-mathematically inclined investor can grasp this vital concept with the following real-world example, which looks at the annual returns of two different domestic stock asset classes— U.S. Large Stocks and REITs—between 1995 and 2002, and then mixes the two of them into a 50/50 portfolio (see Table 3.1).

Table 3.1 Annual Returns of U.S. Large Stocks, REITs, and a 50/50 Mix

	1995	1996	1997	1998	1999	2000	2001	2002	Annualized Return 1995-2002
U.S. Large Stocks	37.07%	22.63%	33.09%	28.68%	20.81%	-9.25%	-12.09%	-22.23%	10.09%
REITs	12.06%	33.84%	19.34%	-15.38%	-1.98%	28.39%	13.16%	4.18%	10.65%
50/50 Mix	24.57%	28.24%	26.22%	6.65%	9.42%	9.57%	0.54%	-9.03%	11.32%

Source: Dimensional Fund Advisors.

Notice how the worst year for U.S. Large Stocks occurred in 2002, with a loss of 22.23 percent, and for REITs in 1998, with a loss of 15.38 percent. Next, note that in 2002, the worst year for the 50/50 portfolio, it lost only 9.03 percent, and further, that it had an overall annualized return greater than either of its two components.

That is because the investor had to adjust the portfolio back to 50/50 at the end of every year. To understand how this works, consider that, by the end of 1995, U.S. Large Stocks had done better than REITs. In order to adjust the portfolio back to 50/50 for the beginning of the next year, the investor had to sell some of the U.S. Large Stocks and buy REITs with the proceeds. The next year, he or she would have done the opposite. This process, called "rebalancing," provides the investor with an automatic buy-low/sell-high bias that over the long run usually—but not always—improves returns.

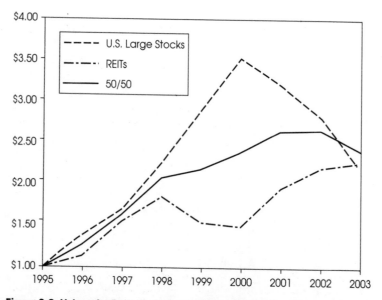

Figure 3.2 Value of a Dollar Invested in U.S. Large Stocks, REITs, and a 50/50 Mix, 1995–2002

Figure 3.2 plots how U.S. Large Stocks, REITs, and the 50/50 portfolio did. It makes clear the smoother ride generated by the 50/50 portfolio. If ever there was a free lunch in investing, this was it: slightly higher returns with much lower risk. How did this happen? In several of the years, U.S. Large Stocks zigged while REITs zagged. This is the essence of portfolio construction: selecting assets that occasionally move in different directions lowers risk, and if the investor is lucky, even raises returns because of the rebalancing process.

> The essence of portfolio construction is the combination of asset classes that move in different directions at least some of the time.

I will admit that I cherry-picked these two asset classes as well as this particular time period, in which the two asset classes often moved in radically different directions yet had nearly the same overall return, to more clearly demonstrate the benefits of diversification. Normally, diversification and rebalancing produce somewhat more subtle benefits, both in terms of risk reduction and return enhancement.

Investors can occasionally *lose* return with rebalancing, as would have occurred in the 1990s with Japanese and U.S. stocks, when the former went nearly straight down, and the latter went nearly straight up. In that case, the investor would have been continually selling what was the best future performer and buying the worst future performer.

These caveats aside, over the long haul portfolio rebalancing, on average, adds value and certainly reduces risk, taking money off the table when a given asset class, or stocks in general, are on a tear and become overvalued.

The U.S. Large Stock/REIT example illustrates another basic principle, which is "the portfolio's the thing": The investor at all costs should avoid becoming overly focused on the components of individual asset classes. For example, between September 2000 and September 2002, U.S. Large Stocks lost nearly half their value; fortunately, this was counterbalanced by gains in REITs. Further, within each of these asset classes were several securities that went bankrupt, even while the overall performance of the asset class was quite agreeable.

As already discussed, the correct response to this divergence in performance of different asset classes is to buy more of the worst-performing ones. Yet some investors cannot avoid obsessing over the sub-par performance of individual portfolio components. Since at any given moment all portfolios will contain one or two underperformers, this sort of behavior will lead to chronic dissatisfaction and worry. If you find that you cannot keep your eyes off the laggards, I strongly recommend that you seek the services of a professional advisor so that you can focus your worries on other areas of your life.

Chasing Rainbows

Is there a way of scientifically picking the very best future allocation, which offers the maximum return for the minimum risk? No, but people still try. In 1952, a University of Chicago finance graduate student, Harry Markowitz, invented a mathematical tool, which subsequently went by the formidable name of "mean-variance analysis," and theoretically allowed investors to compute a so-called "efficient frontier"—all of the portfolios that produced the highest return for a given degree of risk.

Markowitz's technique, which eventually won him the Nobel Prize, requires an accurate prediction of *future* asset class returns and volatility, in addition to the relationships among their returns—the amount of zig versus zag—in each week and year. There is just one slight problem: Making such predictions is not humanly possible. Think about it:

If an investor can successfully predict the best future performer, he does not really need Markowitz's tool, does he? He simply buys that highest-returning asset in each period.

> Be highly skeptical of sophisticated "black box" methods of asset allocation. Garbage in, garbage out.

It took investment professionals quite a while to realize this limitation of mean-variance analysis, and other "black box" techniques for allocating assets. How, then, should you allocate your stock assets? We have already come up with a partial answer: between 80/20 and 60/40 domestic/foreign. A serviceable allocation of your stock assets might be:

70%   Total U.S. Stock Market

30%   Total Foreign Market

Thus, if you have chosen a 60/40 overall stock/bond split, your mix—a balanced portfolio—looks like this:

42%   Total U.S. Stock Market

18%   Total Foreign Market

40%   Total Bond Market

That's it. Done. Does this portfolio seem overly simplistic, even amateurish? Get over it. Over the next few decades, the overwhelming majority of all professional investors will not be able to beat it.

Can this portfolio be improved upon? Probably, but not without more investor effort, and not without some risk of actually making things worse. Still, many investors, including myself, believe that this is worth the work. We will do so in three steps.

First, you might add in a few more asset classes. Probably at the top of most money managers' lists would be REITs. How much? Probably no more than 10 percent of the equity allocation: 6 percent overall of a 60/40 portfolio, for example.

Second, tease apart the foreign stocks into those of developed nations and those of emerging-market nations, which often have very different returns.

Third, consider adding some more risk premiums by increasing exposure to value stocks and to small stocks by dividing the equity asset classes into four corners: large market, small market, large value, and small value. (The large market and small market roughly correspond to Fama and French's "large mid" and "small mid" categories, discussed in Chapter 2.) To get the desired value tilt, ignore the large growth and small growth categories, which have lower expected returns.

Here is how such allocations might look in practice. Again, let's start with the simple 60/40 portfolio described above:

42%   Total U.S. Stock Market
18%   Total Foreign Market
40%   Bonds

Next, add in some REITs and split the foreign stocks into developed and emerging markets portions:

39%   Total U.S. Stock Market
3%   REITs
12%   Foreign Developed Markets
6%   Emerging Markets
40%   Bonds

Already, we are starting to get into significant practical portfolio management issues. In the first place, the fund minimum for the Vanguard REIT Fund is $3,000, which implies a portfolio size of at least $100,000. You could buy a smaller amount of the asset class in a so-called exchange-traded fund, or ETF, but these incur brokerage commissions and spreads that would substantially reduce the return of such a tiny position. Another practical problem is that about 2 percent of the Total Stock Market Fund already consists of REITs, meaning that the actual REIT allocation of this portfolio will be about 3.8 percent.

Finally, if you have a large portfolio, in excess of $250,000–$500,000, and you can handle the complexity, then you might want to split your domestic and foreign developed market allocation into a small- and value-weighted "four corners portfolio":

- 10%   U.S. Large Market
- 9%   U.S. Small Market
- 10%   U.S. Large Value
- 10%   U.S. Small Value
- 3%   REITs
- 3%   Foreign Developed Large Market
- 3%   Foreign Developed Small Market
- 3%   Foreign Developed Large Value
- 3%   Foreign Developed Small Value
- 3%   Emerging Markets Large Market
- 3%   Emerging Markets Large Value
- 40%   Bonds

These three models are most definitely not hard-and-fast recommendations. They only serve to illustrate how the asset allocation process works in the real world of investing. You are going to have to personalize your allocation to your age, overall risk tolerance, portfolio size, and tolerance for complexity.

The previous portfolio contains most of the asset classes that anyone with a portfolio of under a million dollars might reasonably want to own. Are there any other asset classes you should consider?

The asset class that has received the most attention over the past several years is commodities futures. (Or at least they did before falling off a cliff in late 2008.)

Two things are wrong with this asset class. First, its future returns will likely be low—certainly much lower than they have been in the past; commodities are what I call an "asset class du jour," on everyone's financial lips. This is a real warning sign, since when everyone owns something, few buyers may be left to push up the price. Second, I just do not trust any of the commodities funds, or the companies offering them. I will explain exactly why in Chapter 5, which covers the brokerage and mutual fund industries.

The stocks of gold, silver, and platinum mining companies provide much of the same diversification benefits as commodities futures. I am less enthusiastic about them now than I was a few years ago for two reasons. First, my old favorite in this area, the Vanguard Precious Metals and Mining Fund, has broadened its charter to invest in companies that mine base metals (mainly aluminum, copper, and lead) and other natural resources, and this significantly decreases its diversification value. Second, gold and gold stocks have also become an asset class du jour, with high recent returns and a good deal of publicity. Unless you are going on the lam, buying gold bullion itself, gold coins, or an ETF that invests in them, is rarely a good idea. The long-term, real return of the yellow metal itself is zero—an ounce of it bought a fine men's suit in Shakespeare's time, and still does today. In addition, gold yields no dividend and incurs storage costs.

Another asset class worthy of consideration is international REITs—property companies in Europe, Asia, and

Australia. Like U.S. REITs, they have suffered recent massive price falls, and consequently yield dividends in excess of 8 percent. They may also offer even more diversification than their domestic cousins. Their only drawback is that they are only available in passive funds to independent small investors in ETF form, and thus incur commissions and spreads. Since this asset class should not constitute more than a few percent of anyone's assets, I do not recommend including it in a portfolio unless its size is at least several hundred thousand dollars, and you can tolerate a highly complex mix of assets.

Almost as important as what asset classes you choose are the nuts and bolts of your portfolio locations. For example, the lion's share of your savings may be located in sheltered retirement accounts, such as a 401(k) or an IRA. In this case, you can own almost any asset class, without regard to the tax consequences.

Alternatively, your portfolio might consist entirely of taxable accounts, with little or no sheltered retirement assets. In this situation, it would be inadvisable to own high-yield bonds, since all of their long-term return comes from dividends taxed at the ordinary income rate. Conversely, you might also want to cant an all-taxable portfolio toward domestic and foreign large-market equity funds, which are highly tax-efficient, and the bond portion toward municipal securities.

Summary

- A balanced portfolio consists of significant allocations to both stocks and bonds. This minimizes your chances of dying poor. Investing too much in risky assets could have dire consequences in the event of a long-lasting market failure, but so does investing too much in safe assets that will fail to grow your portfolio enough to sustain your retirement needs. Invest in stocks only that money that you will not need for at least a decade or two.

- The overall stock/bond split in your retirement portfolio depends primarily upon your age and tolerance for risk.

- Simple portfolios, consisting of just two stock asset classes (a domestic and a foreign total stock market fund) and one bond asset class can perform surprisingly well. More complex portfolios, particularly those with value and small stock emphasis, may have higher returns, but come at the cost of time and effort. Further, because of fund minimums, complex allocations are suitable only for larger portfolios.

CHAPTER

The Enemy in the Mirror

Nearly every student pilot, at some point early in the training process, has the following experience: The instructor coaxes him down onto a short, grass landing strip bounded at either end by high trees. It is a little scary, but the student figures the instructor, who has flown thousands of hours, must know what he is doing.

After debriefing the approach and landing, it is time to take off again. The student knows the procedure—apply full power and pull back on the control yoke to get the fragile nose wheel off the rough ground. Soon, the student, instructor, and plane are bumping down the field, gaining speed, but far more slowly than normal on the soft, uneven turf.

As the seconds drag by, the trees at the end of the runway loom closer and taller. At long last, the aircraft looses the bonds of earth, and the student yanks back even harder on the yoke to clear the firs and alders that threaten to consume the tin can that surrounds him and his instructor.

Calmly, the instructor tells him "My plane" and pushes the yoke forward, and the plane's nose with it, *down*, and aims straight at the trees. Which, of course, is the correct thing to do; when the student pulled the struggling plane off the ground, it had not gained enough airspeed to climb.

95

Only by flying level for a few more seconds could the plane accelerate to proper flying speed and successfully clear the trees.

The difference between the behavior of the student and of the instructor was simple: the former responded *reflexively*, driven purely by gut, emotional instinct, while the latter acted *reflectively* and used his knowledge of aerodynamics and logical facilities to save the student from paying for a new aircraft and extensive orthopedic procedures for two people.

The lecture hall provides a colleague, Jason Zweig, with an even better example of this phenomenon. Intentionally, he will drone on for a few minutes about the minutiae of behavioral finance and lull his audience into a light stupor. He then deftly reaches into a bag at his feet and tosses a rubber rattlesnake into the front row. This unwelcome projectile always elicits the same reaction from those in its immediate trajectory: horror and recoil followed a few seconds later by sheepish laughter.

The reflexive reaction of his victims is a nearly instantaneous rush of adrenaline and horror, hardwired into our brains by our evolutionary heritage: Snake!! A few seconds later, the reflective parts of our brains compute easily: Mr. Zweig certainly did not pack a rattlesnake into his flight luggage and smuggle it into this ballroom, and besides, he is too nice a guy to throw one into an audience. Ergo, the rattlesnake is not real. (Mr. Zweig's voyage over the past few years into neuroeconomics has informed many finance professionals, including myself, about this field. If this chapter intrigues you, I cannot recommend his recent book, *Your Money and Your Brain*, strongly enough.)[1]

Reflection takes time and effort; reflexion (were there such a word) happens automatically and nearly instantaneously, the product of millions of years of evolution in an environment in which the avoidance of snakes conferred real survival value.

In every field of human endeavor, whether it is flying, medicine, or armed combat, this reflexive/reflective split cleaves the world into amateurs and professionals, the former driven by their emotions, the latter by calculation and logic. Investors also need to master their emotions to avoid flying into the financial trees and dodging rubber investment snakes. This chapter examines the major dysfunctional, gut responses that the investing brain is prone to and prescribes remedies. In short, it describes how you can change from a reflexive investing amateur into a reflective professional.

> Nothing is more likely to make you poor than your own emotions; nothing is more likely to save your finances than learning how to use cool, dispassionate reason to hold these emotions in check.

Inner Demons

You have no doubt heard that investment is all about fear and greed—what Keynes famously called the "animal spirits." Well, that eccentric, outrageous Cambridge don knew what he was talking about. In recent years, psychologists and neuroscientists have learned a great deal about the biological basis of these two emotions, and wherever possible this chapter relates some of this exciting new work to the age-old story of financial foolishness.

First, a little neuroanatomy. Over the past several decades, scientists have actually been able to locate the two systems within our brains that mediate fear and greed. These reflexive centers reside primarily in the so-called "limbic system," whose nerve cells, or neurons, lie near the center of the brain. Were you to divide your skull exactly into symmetric right and left halves along a vertical plane, most of the limbic system would lie on or near it on either side. In front of the brain—just behind each eye—sit a pair of neuron groups called the nuclei accumbens. It would not be too much of an oversimplification to call these tiny structures the brain's "anticipation center." They are most electrically and metabolically active during the *anticipation* of eating, sex, agreeable social activity, and most importantly for our purposes, financial reward. If greed resides any single place in the brain—an assignment that neurologists and neuroscientists are loathe to make about any cognitive function—it is here.*

It really is true: The anticipation is better than the pleasure. Researchers have found that the nuclei accumbens respond much more to the prospect of reward than to the reward itself. Further, it is all the same to the nuclei accumbens, which respond nearly identically to the prospect of food, sex, social contact, cocaine, or financial gain.

The nuclei accumbens are particularly sensitive to the *pattern* of stimuli. If every Friday at noon you are served your favorite lunch, these tiny structures will be happily firing away at 11:55 A.M. If your portfolio has been doing well lately, the same will happen each morning at 9:29 A.M. when you turn on CNBC and see Maria Bartiromo's winsome visage smiling back at you from the stock exchange floor.

Continuing the anatomy lesson, two symmetric pathways fan outward from the midline limbic apparatus toward your temples, ending in the amygdalae (singular: amygdala). These two structures, whose name derives from the Latin word for walnut, that they resemble, mediate some of our deepest negative emotions: revulsion, fear, and loathing. Again, it is not too much of an oversimplification to call them our "fear centers." It is of no small significance that

---

*Although the singular term nucleus accumbens is more commonly used, from now on I employ the plural form to avoid confusion; the image I wish to evoke is a pair of greedy glowing coals, one behind each eye.

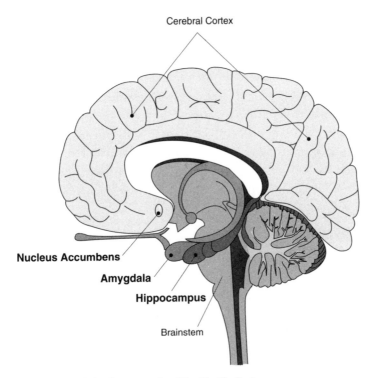

Figure 4.1 The Major Components of the Limbic System

adjacent to them lie the hippocampi, which encode our memories.

Beyond the evolutionary level of, say, frogs, the limbic systems of most vertebrate species look pretty much the same, and probably serve the same function: the rapid interpretation of and reaction to environmental stimuli—no conscious thought necessary. This system, along with the brainstem, that lies below it, is often referred to as the hindbrain, or more colloquially as the "reptilian brain," a not inaccurate metaphor for the level at which many investors operate.

What differentiates primates, and particularly humans, from the rest of the vertebrate species is the enormous size of the outer covering of the brain adjacent to the skull, the "cortex" (deriving from the Latin word for outer shell, husk, or bark). Again, to the extent that we can assign any activity to a given neuroanatomic structure, it is here that conscious thought, that is, our reflective brain, resides.

Nearly every time we invest, our cortex, where we consciously calculate and reflect, battles with our limbic system, the repository of our instincts and emotions. The extent to which we succeed depends in no small part on how well the cortex keeps the limbic system in check.

Behaving Badly

Let me be clear: Our emotions define our humanity, what binds us to our family, friends, and neighbors. Without them, we are soulless, heartless automatons, devoid of meaning or purpose. But in the world of finance, they are death itself.

Human beings are supremely social creatures. Cut us off from friends and family, and we become depressed and listless; continue the isolation, and we will get sick and die. Epidemiologists have long known that both social isolation and loss of status lead to increased rates of hypertension, cardiovascular disease, and early death.[2]

Although our friends, family, and neighbors can make us emotionally and physically healthy, they can simultaneously make us fiscally sick. We cannot help but be affected by the fear and greed of those around us; our empathy with and envy of others stimulates our amygdalae and nuclei accumbens. I have long been troubled to observe that caring, emotionally intelligent people often make the worst investors, as they become too overwhelmed by the feelings of others to think rationally about the investment process. Contrariwise, the most callous, selfish, and disdainful people, who can easily tune out the emotions of others, respond less to the fear and greed of the investing masses and thus regularly make the best investment decisions. In the following pages we will first identify how some of the most noble aspects of human nature generate maladaptive financial behaviors, and then learn how to build walls around them when we put on our investing hats.

What, then, are these adverse reflexive behaviors, bred into our psyches over the eons, that make us poor?

We Crave Easy-to-Understand Narratives

We will start with perhaps the most admirable of human emotions, our desire to comprehend the world around us. Psychologists and historians have long known that humans are hardwired to understand events in narrative form; man truly is the primate that tells stories. As put so well by the late Kurt Vonnegut, "Tiger got to hunt, Bird got to fly, Man have to ask, 'Why, why, why?' Tiger got to sleep, Bird got to land, Man have to say he understand."[3] When a problem becomes too logically or mathematically complex to grasp easily, humans default back into this evolutionarily ancient story-telling mode.

The trouble is that in finance, things can get complex in a hurry. For example, imagine you are a physician who enjoys researching and purchasing individual stocks. Further, you think that you know something about the pharmaceutical industry; after all, you prescribe medicines all day long, and you know what works. Might this give you a leg up on other investors?

Theoretically, yes. But in the real world, physicians nearly always screw it up. The proper way to approach this problem would be to evaluate all of the company's products, then estimate their revenues, costs, and resultant cash flows every year for the next several decades. Next, since those cash flows will occur in the future, you must arrive at their "present value"—what those future flows are worth *now*—by reducing their value by a so-called discount rate that is different for each year. The sum of all these so-called discounted cash flows for all the company's present and future products defines the actual "intrinsic value" of the stock, in other words, what it is actually worth *today*. If the current market price is below it, then you might consider buying it. (The Gordon Equation falls directly out of this calculation. For those who are interested, see the Math Detail on pages 29–32.)

Sounds difficult? Well, it is; it is also the bread and butter of the trained securities analyst. What does everyone else do, including 100 percent of physicians? They respond to such overwhelming complexities as have humans since prehistoric times: They tell stories.

In the case of our hapless physician, the narrative unfolds something like this: Druggy LaRoche Pharmaceuticals has just come out with a world-beating antibiotic, threeblindmycin. My patients love it, and I think it's the next Viagra. I'm buying as much of the stock as I can get my hands on. Discounted cash flow? Intrinsic value versus current stock price? Don't bother me with silly details.

The financial institutions on the other side of his stock purchases, naturally, have done the hard math and have decided to sell their Druggy LaRoche stock to our storytelling physician. (If our doctor is particularly unlucky, he will find himself buying his shares from a Druggy LaRoche executive.)

This toxic narrative brew often acquires further appeal from one of the financial world's signal characteristics: the extreme amount of random noise inherent in it. So while the odds are stacked against the physician, he is not doomed to fail, at least not at first. The worst thing, in fact, that could happen to him would be to benefit from beginner's luck and make a bundle on his first trade. Mistaking luck for skill, he will double up on his next purchase, and maybe even get lucky again and double up yet one more time. But however well things will turn out for him initially, he will eventually lose his money.

Let's return to the current investing climate. Today's narrative is all too apparent: "The world economy is imploding, and corporate profits will collapse along with it. Stocks will become worthless." Yet, the Gordon Equation computation of expected returns shown in Chapter 1 clearly shows that even if earnings disappear for a few years, future equity returns should be reasonable, particularly for REITs and foreign stocks. Similarly, bonds of all stripes—except everybody's current favorite, Treasury securities—should also do just fine, as long as the investor keeps maturities relatively short (less than five years) to mitigate the risk of unexpected high inflation.

> Learn to automatically mistrust simple narrative explanations of complex economic or financial events.

By contrast, a mere decade ago the prevalent narrative was far more upbeat: "The Internet changes everything." This exciting new technology was going to drive our economy, corporate profits, and stock prices into the stratosphere, and we were all going to get rich. The only problem was that when economists looked for hard evidence of this miracle in the macroeconomic data, it just was not there.

Popular finance books provide an excellent barometer of uninformed narrative-borne public sentiment, since ambitious financial authors tend to pander to it. One group of researchers indeed found that when the bookshelves turn bearish (*The Crash of 1979*, published in 1976, and *The Great Depression of 1990*, published in 1985), stocks had above-average future returns. The opposite happened when bullish titles (most infamously, the already-mentioned *Dow 36,000*, published near the peak of the 1999 bubble) lined the shelves.[4] When this title reaches bookstores, it will undoubtedly be surrounded by several variants of *The Crash of 2011.*

We Want to Be Entertained

Not only do humans like to tell stories, they want to be amused by them. Owning shares of Netflix is much more enjoyable than owning, say, Consolidated Edison or Federal Screw Works.

Many, if not most, of our purchases of both consumer goods and investment vehicles can be broken into two parts: entertainment and investing. Consider a lottery ticket: Your one dollar purchase at the local convenience store is in reality a marketable security with a one-week expected return of about minus 50 percent. Clearly, a miserable asset class if ever there was one.

Yet, folks buy these things. Why? Because a lottery ticket's return is only partly financial. What it lacks in strictly fiscal terms, it makes up for in entertainment value. In other words, the heady but short-lived fun of dreaming about spending the rest of your life in Maui is the happy job of your greed center, the nuclei accumbens; this happy diversion supplements the low return. Taking this line of reasoning to its logical extreme, a theater ticket is an investment that compensates for its minus 100 percent return with a very high entertainment value.

As already alluded to, some investments entertain more than others. Initial public offerings (IPOs) of the stock of exciting new companies come most readily to mind. A wealth of research demonstrates that IPOs have, in general, lousy returns with very high risk. This is not a new observation; three-quarters of a century ago, investment legend Ben Graham, in his seminal *Security Analysis*, wondered why folks bought IPOs. Here is why: It is so much more fun taking a chance on finding the next Amazon.com or Microsoft than owning a doggy industrial company. In short, IPOs are the investment equivalent of a lottery ticket, with high entertainment value and low investment returns.

A few decades ago, I enjoyed a dinner at a local franchise of a well-known chain of Asian restaurants. Impressed with the food and service, I researched the stock and saw that it was trading at a ludicrously expensive price relative to its earnings. Clearly, because the business had such high visibility, and because ethnic restaurant chains were a hot item in the equity markets in those days, millions of other investors had already gotten the same idea. Tens of thousands of happy diners bid up the stock's price to the point that it was likely to (and eventually did) produce low returns going forward.

> If you want excitement in your life, it is far safer and cheaper to take up skydiving than to seek it in your investment portfolio.

Thus, the more public visibility a company has, and the more well-known and entertaining its story, the lower its future returns are likely to be. By contrast, it is the most obscure companies in the most unglamorous businesses that often have the highest returns.

We Are Too Easily Frightened

If you are an unsuccessful investor, blame the walnut-shaped tangle of neurons just inside your temples, your amygdalae. Think of them as your central server for fight or flight—the first place in your brain that lights up when you encounter a snake, a potential assailant, or a falling Dow.[5]

As recently as a few centuries ago, in a world of very real physical threats, our amygdalae served us well. Monkeys that have had their amygdalae removed lose their fear of human handlers, and amygdalae-less mice will happily play with cats.

However, in the safety-conscious, modern, postindustrial West, our amygdalae are in many ways a mixed blessing, sending out false alarm after false alarm: alar in the apples, allergens in the atmosphere, and killer bees heading north from Mexico.

In no field of human endeavor do our amygdalae betray us more than in investing. Investors would possibly be better off without them, as shown by a series of experiments performed by a group of economists and neuroscientists at Stanford, Carnegie Mellon, and Iowa Universities. This work simultaneously gets to the heart of both the investment process and how humans respond dysfunctionally to financial loss, so I describe their work in some detail.

The research group studied 15 patients with damage to their amygdalae, as well as to two other cortical brain centers associated with the processing of unpleasant emotional stimuli: the orbitofrontal cortex and insula. (These last two areas respond more to the unpleasant memories of fear-producing stimuli than to the actual stimuli themselves.) For comparison, they also studied the responses of two other groups: normal controls and patients with damage to other parts of their brains.

The experimenters gave each subject $20 of play money, which at the end of the experiment was exchanged for the real thing. The design was simple, consisting of 20 rounds of coin tosses. Before each, the subjects decided whether to "invest" $1 in the upcoming flip. If it came up tails, the subjects won $2.50; if it came up heads, they lost the $1 investment.

If subjects decided to invest in none of the rounds, they were assured of keeping their original $20. If they invested in all the rounds, they would win, on average, $25.

The experimenters thus assumed that "it would behoove the participants to invest in all the rounds."

Overall, the patients with damage to their emotional circuitry bet in 84 percent of the rounds versus only 58 percent of the normal participants and 61 percent of the participants with brain damage not involving their emotional circuitry. Even more interesting, after losing a round, the emotionally impaired group invested with about the same 84 percent frequency as after a winning round, but the percentage of bets placed by the other two groups fell to 41 and 37 percent, respectively. In other words, not only did the two control groups bet less frequently than the emotionally impaired group, but they also were even less likely to bet after a losing round.

The authors concluded that damage to the brain's emotional circuitry, by blunting negative response to losing money, enabled emotionally impaired subjects faced with typical investment-type decisions to "make more advantageous decisions than normal subjects."[6]

Well, not so fast. It is certainly true that the emotionally impaired group did not change their betting behavior after a losing round, a far more rational response than that of the other two groups, which when stung by a losing round tended not to bet on the next one.

It is also true that carefully performed psychosurgery would probably improve the personalities of many investment professionals. However, the case for improving investment results is less clear. Remember, by betting on all rounds it was possible to come out with less than the safe $20 by tossing less than eight tails. The odds of coming out behind by betting on all rounds were 13 percent, while the risk premium for doing so was only $5 (the difference between the $25 expected return of betting on all of the rounds and the $20 risk-free return of betting on none).

This is a fair representation of the investment process. What is interesting is that the experimenters automatically made the assumption that it was rational to go for the $5 risk premium in the face of a 13 percent chance of coming out with less than the assured $20 of the risk-free, no-bet strategy. In truth, whether this risk/reward tradeoff is indeed rational all depends on how risk-averse the investor or the experimental subject is.

Thus, all that we can say for sure is that the emotionally damaged subjects were more risk tolerant than the controls—probably not a bad thing—and that they did not change their investment strategy after losing money, which is definitely a good thing.

Because it arises from our fast-moving limbic system, fear is also a short-term phenomenon. It makes little sense that we should care about a bad day or a bad year in the stock market if it provides us with good long-term returns. But because of the importance of our limbic systems, we care—very, very much—about short-term losses.

We cannot help it: That is the way we are hardwired. Behavioral studies show that, in emotional terms, a loss of $1 approximately offsets a gain of $2; in the unlovely language of economics, the negative utility of losses is twice that of the positive utility of gains.

Let's see how this plays out in the real world of investing. Between 1929 and 2008, the Dow Jones Industrial Average rose 51.6 percent of days and fell 48.4 percent of days. If one day of losses offsets two days of gains in our psyches, then on average we would feel horrible, since the number of gaining and losing days is nearly equal. Even worse than checking your portfolio every day is watching CNBC, with its anxiety-causing minute-by-minute stream of bad news.

Decrease the intake of financial data to once per month, and things improve only slightly: 57.5 percent winning months versus 42.5 percent losing months, but this still falls short of the two-to-one barrier. Even at a one-year observation interval, with 52 winning years and 28 losing years, we do not quite get to hedonic break-even; only when we check our portfolios less than once per year do we finally clear the grim psychological two-to-one hurdle. Behavioral economists call this dysfunctional overemphasis on the short term "risk aversion myopia" and have determined that investors seem to behave as if their time horizons are approximately one year—almost precisely where the two-to-one hedonic hurdle lives.[7] How many investors do you think are capable of looking at the market less than once per year?

We Make Too Many Analogies

Closely related to the narrative error is "representativeness," which refers to the human tendency to transfer characteristics across categories. We have already encountered one example of this with the good company/good stock fallacy: You would think that the stocks of glamorous growth companies would clock higher returns, but they do not. The shares of doggy value companies do better, if for no other reason that they *must* offer a higher return to induce investors to buy them.

The same thing that is true about individual companies and their stocks is also true of the economies and stock markets of entire nations. When you invest abroad, should you not favor those economies that are growing most rapidly? Actually, no. It turns out that this naive strategy will cost you plenty. For example, in Chapter 2 we saw that, since 1993, China has had one of the world's highest economic growth rates—at times exceeding 10 percent per year. Yet between 1993 and 2008, its stock market has *lost* 3.3 percent per year. We also have already learned that, to a lesser degree, the same is true for the other great economic success stories of the past few decades, the Asian tigers—Korea, Singapore, Malaysia, Indonesia, Taiwan, and Thailand—which since 1988 have all had lower returns than in the low-growth United States.[8]

By contrast, no major nation has seen its relative economic and geopolitical position fall farther during the twentieth century than the United Kingdom. In 1900, Britannia not only ruled the waves, but the world's financial markets as well. In 2000, by contrast, it was little more than an open-air theme park playing second fiddle to the American hegemon. Once again, this had no impact on British equity returns, which were among the world's highest during the twentieth century.[9]

> Nations with the most rapidly growing economies often have the lowest stock returns.

More systematic data confirm the above anecdotal suggestion that good economies tend to be bad stock markets, and vice versa.[10] What is going on here? These puzzling results defy easy explanation, but in my opinion, three factors contribute to the good economy/bad market phenomenon.

Just as the prices of stocks of poorly performing companies must fall to the point where they will entice investors with higher future returns, the same probably happens at the country level. In 2007, everyone wanted to own that year's darlings, the so-called BRIC countries: Brazil, Russia, India, and China. Relatively few were attracted to the less glamorous markets of Europe, Japan, and perhaps the United States. Consequently, just as with unglamorous stocks, unglamorous stock markets should have higher returns. Indeed, in 2008 the developed world's markets fell far less than those in the BRIC countries, which, if history is any guide, should continue to have poor relative returns in the long term.

As explained in Chapter 1, because companies, like people, die and are replaced with new ones, new shares are constantly being sold and dilute out the pool of existing shares. In many foreign countries, particularly in Asia, the rate of new share issuance is especially high. This reduces per-share earnings and dividends, which in turn erodes overall stock returns.[11]

Finally, in many developing markets, governments do not protect shareholders from the rapacity of management as well as in nations with more established legal systems. In other words, in these countries, management and controlling shareholders find it disturbingly easy to loot a company. Even more bluntly, a nation that does not protect its children from lead-contaminated toys will likely not protect its foreign shareholders.

We Extrapolate the Recent Past Too Far into the Future

In the lingo of the evolutionary psychologist, humans are "pattern-seeking primates" that tend to perceive order where none exists. A hundred thousand years ago, if seeing a flash of yellow and black stripes in your peripheral vision was followed by the gruesome death of one of your companions, you would do well to associate those two events.

By contrast, modern life presents human beings with a much more statistically noisy environment, and few areas are more rich and random than finance. You say Bill Miller has beaten the market every year like clockwork for the past 15 years, and it is a slam dunk he will continue to do so? Did the fact that, since the fall of 2008, you did nothing but lose money in the stock market month after month make you pessimistic about future equity returns? Conversely, did the relentless real estate boom that began in the late 1990s lead you to believe that houses never lost value?

If you answered yes to these questions, do not despair; you are human or, more accurately, a pattern-seeking primate whose emotions instinctively respond, whether you want them to or not, to the financial environment. Cognitive psychologists call this tendency to extrapolate the immediate past indefinitely into the future and to ignore the longer-term data "recency," a behavioral pattern that seems designed right into our limbic systems.

> Nothing lasts forever: More often than not, recent extraordinary economic and financial events tend to reverse.

It turns out that our nuclei accumbens activate strongly to repeated rewards. Similarly, when neuroscientists implant electrodes into the nuclei accumbens of rats, they can actually record this anticipation-related activity.[12] In fact, our brains will respond strongly to just two similar events in a row, and even more strongly to three or more in a row.[13] Consider that in a series of three coin flips, three successive heads or tails will happen 25 percent of the time; in a series of five coin flips, three-in-a-row will occur with 50 percent probability; and in a series of 10, it is a virtual certainty. In a data-rich modern world, it is no wonder that we are constantly alerting ourselves to spurious patterns. In the words of financial author Nicholas Nassim Taleb, we are "fooled by randomness."

We Are All Better Than Average

Every year, behavioral economist Terry Odean hands out a questionnaire to his MBA students at Berkeley that asks them to rate their driving ability relative to their classmates. Typically, at least one-half of the class rates itself in the top quarter, and one-quarter rates itself in the top 10 percent.

Only a few rate themselves below average; this, of course, cannot possibly be true.

One year, however, a female student did rate herself below average, and Odean asked her why. She replied that she was going to place herself in the top quarter until she realized that in the past year she had been in two accidents, had received three speeding tickets, and was in the process of having her license revoked. (Only one student has ever rated himself in the bottom 10 percent: It turned out he was from a foreign country and did not drive.)[14]

Not only do we think we are all better than average drivers, but we also believe that we are better looking and better liked than others think we are, and are more likely to succeed at business than others. Overconfidence even spills into the hereafter: A recent poll shows that 64 percent of Americans believe they are going to heaven, versus only 0.5 percent who will be traveling in the opposite direction when the time comes.[15]

As we saw in the introduction, we also believe that we are better than average at investing, that we will earn higher investment returns than others, that we can pick mutual fund managers successfully, and that we can predict the movements of the market, all in spite of overwhelming evidence to the contrary.

> You are not as good looking, as charming, or as good a driver as you think you are. The same goes for your investing abilities. In an environment filled with incredibly smart, hard-working, and well-informed participants, the smartest trading strategy is not to trade at all.

The degree of inappropriate overconfidence on the part of some individuals can be awe-inspiring. In 1993, Orange County Treasurer Robert L. Citron single-handedly caused the largest municipal bankruptcy in U.S. history with a complex series of derivatives bets that interest rates would fall or stay flat. When asked what would happen if interest rates *rose*, he replied that they would not. Asked how he knew, he retorted, "I am one of the largest investors in America. I know these things."[16] Mr. Citron was obviously unaware of John Kenneth Galbraith's famous dictum that there were only two kinds of people in the world—those who don't know where interest rates were headed, and those who don't know that they don't know. Almost all of us know small-bore versions of Mr. Citron, most often chronically broke acquaintances who regularly regale others with tales of their investment prowess.

Interestingly, the most outrageous instances of overconfidence and grandiosity are seen in patients in the throes of the manic phase of bipolar disorder; conversely, those suffering from major depression often have the most accurate self-assessments of their own abilities. In light of these observations, it is difficult to avoid the conclusion that we require a certain amount of self-delusion in order to maintain our self-esteem.

We Need to Keep Up with the Joneses

Many, if not most, animal species exhibit some sort of pecking order, and humans are no exception. The evolutionary roots of this behavior are obvious: In an environment with scarce food and resources, only the strongest and most capable survive, mate, and reproduce. A pecking order, whether in birds or humans, provides a handy shorthand for ascertaining who is most evolutionarily fit. In many animal species, the lowest-ranking males often shut down their reproductive systems and become physically inactive, while a few alpha males collect most of the female partners.

Modern societies—at least those outside the Muslim world—have outlawed polygyny, and only recently in human evolutionary history have those at the bottom of the social scale been able to easily acquire a mate and reproduce. But we still cannot escape our evolutionary heritage; at all costs we must keep up appearances. In the words of Karl Marx:

> A house may be large or small; as long as the surrounding houses are equally small it satisfies all social demands for a dwelling. If a palace rises besides the little house, the little house shrinks into a hut.[17]

In America, as the old joke goes, envy is your neighbor's bigger house and car; in England, it's your neighbor's having tea with the Queen; in France, it's your neighbor's better-looking lover; and in Russia, it's wishing your neighbor's cow was dead.

Well, all over the world, in finance, envy is your neighbor owning a glamorous stock or hedge fund that you do not, or having a money manager or advisor you cannot get. Unfortunately, lusting after glamorous investments can damage your finances at least as much as hankering after a sexual partner, car, or house that you cannot afford.

One of medicine's little secrets is that wealthy people, by fragmenting their care through doctor shopping, often get worse treatment than ordinary people, usually by winding up with charlatan "celebrity physicians." The same is true in finance, where the wealthy have access to managers and investment vehicles not available to plain folks, particularly hedge funds, limited partnerships, and the like. As the Madoff affair and the recent disasters in alternative investment vehicles have amply demonstrated, in almost all cases, the rich would be far better off investing with the hoi polloi in plain-vanilla, low-cost index funds.

The "celebrity physician" analogue of the investment world is the hedge fund, which typically charges "two and twenty": a 2 percent management fee and 20 percent of returns. So if your hedge fund makes 10 percent per year, the fees alone will total 4 percent per year. That's just for starters, since these funds also incur significant transactional costs and are usually packaged through advisors and/or so-called "funds of funds," both of which charge yet another layer of fees. By the time all is said and done, the typical hedge fund investor is flying into about a 7 percent per year headwind—a handicap that not even Warren Buffett could overcome. In a taxable account, hedge funds are even more of a disaster, since most of their returns come in the form of short-term capital gains, which are taxed as ordinary income. One more sobering thought to consider about hedge funds: They disappear faster than taco chips at a Super Bowl party. Of 600 that registered with the government in 1996, just one-quarter still operated by 2004.[18]

Bargain-Basement Psychotherapy

What, then, can you do to escape the psychological poorhouse that human evolution has seemingly condemned you to? I do not recommend that you become an automaton, suffer a traumatic brain injury, or undergo a bout of major depression, but you can approach each of the above behavioral flaws systematically. While most psychotherapy comes with a stiff price tag, the financial head-shrinking that I describe below will cost you nothing at all and pay off handsomely in the long term.

Beware of Glib Narrative Explanations

The reason that "guru" is such a popular word is because "charlatan" is so hard to spell. So much uncertainty surrounds the markets that it is impossible for even the best informed observers to compute whether at any point in time they should invest in a given stock, sector, or market, or when to be in or out of the market. In recent years, the darlings of the story-telling crowd have been commodities funds and BRIC (Brazil, Russia, India, and China) country stocks, with disastrous results for those who read and listened to their claptrap.

Dare to Be Dull

Resign yourself to the fact that you can have either the sizzle or the steak, but you cannot have both. If it is excitement you seek, take up bungee jumping. If you want to be entertained, go to New York for a month's worth of Broadway shows. I can guarantee you that the former will be safer, and the latter less expensive, than seeking amusement in your investments.

If done properly, successful investing entertains as much as watching clothes tumble in the dryer window. Always remember that the more exciting a given stock or asset class is, the more likely it is to be over-owned, overpriced, and destined for low future returns.

In most years, a portfolio designed to minimize your chances of dying poor will spread among so many securities and asset classes that its performance will not do much to quicken the pulse. If you do feel compelled to seek excitement in finance—and I do not recommend it—hive off a small portion of your portfolio with which to amuse yourself. Segregate this account, which should be no larger than 10 percent of your nest egg, from the rest of your portfolio, and never add to it. When it is gone, it is gone, and hopefully with it the thrill of stock picking.

Get into Financial Shape

It is a fact: Some investors are in much better financial shape than others. No, I do not mean their salaries, job security, net worth, credit card balances, or mortgage debt. I am talking about their *emotional* condition: the ability to bear risk and loss.

Eighty years ago, John Maynard Keynes put it best:

> I do not feel that selling at very low prices is a remedy for having failed to sell at high ones. . . . I would say that it is from time to time the duty of the serious investor to accept the depreciation of his holdings with equanimity and without reproaching himself.[19]

Keynes was surely speaking to the recent financial Armageddon. As we saw in Chapter 1, this carnage has left the prices of equities around the world at near bargain-basement levels. And yet, most investors will avoid buying more stocks, the most rational response to this global fire-sale.

For some reason, we do not purchase securities in the same way we buy other things. When the price of strawberries rises to $8 per pound in January, we forego them, and when they are virtually being given away at the farmers' market in June, we load up. Not so with stocks: The higher the price, the more attractive they seem; and the lower they have fallen, the more we are repulsed.

Buy low and sell high: these words roll so easily off the tongue. Yet most investors cannot manage it because they lack the emotional stamina to do what needs to be done. Like the out-of-condition athlete, they are in lousy *financial* shape.

From the perspective of investment discipline, the years from 2003 to 2006 were the emotional equivalent of a non-stop beer-and-pizza party: If an investor could organize a two-car parade, he or she could earn ludicrously high returns. Then, just as suddenly, the party-goers were thrown out onto the street and forced to run a marathon; few will make it to the end standing.

How, then, do you keep yourself in tip-top financial shape in order to reach your retirement finish line? The same way you would prepare for any athletic event, with a rigorous, disciplined training approach. A word of warning: This takes years, and in some cases, decades.

Your primary training tool is the rebalancing process, which forces you to sell high in the good years and to buy low when there is blood in the streets. In the really bad years, such as 2008–2009, this will mean pouring large amounts into falling equities, when your friends and family are running around like decapitated poultry. This will feel terrible; most grizzled veterans will tell you that the best purchases are often made when they feel they are about to throw up.

Do this regularly and long enough and you will gradually learn that the most profitable acquisitions are usually made at the worst of times. Stocks never become cheap unless bad news abounds, and slowly but surely you will become accustomed to buying low at these times. That is to say, you will find yourself in good "financial condition." If you are especially lucky, you will be able to perform successfully in the most exciting round of the financial Olympics, the historic bear markets in which the ownership of stocks reverts to their rightful owners: the taut-bellied, hard-muscled, long-term investors with the stamina to buy under the blackest skies.

A neuroscientist might put this message a different way: Learn to recognize the panicked messages from your amygdalae as the frantic shrieks of your reptilian brain, which wants nothing more than to make you poor. Learn also to translate the primitive language of our evolutionary past from the walnut-shaped devils inside your head into the argot of the modern financial present. When you turn on CNBC and your limbic system yells "Snake!" understand what that really means: If ever there was a time to buy, it just might be now. By the same token, learn to recognize the cocaine-like rush from the glowing coals of your nuclei accumbens as the siren song of lost fortune. When the not-so-subtle message from CNBC is "Buy!" hold on tight to your wallet.

In my experience, it is the ability to ignore these dysfunctional instinctive responses that determines, as much as anything else, which investors wind up with the highest returns. Remember, the limbic system has the attention span of a two-year-old, obsessing on daily changes in market prices. So during market declines, shut it down. The sooner you turn off CNBC, get out into the bright sunshine, and take a walk, the better you will feel about your investments.

By all means, enjoy contact with your family and friends; just do not, under any circumstances, discuss finance with them during severe market declines. It will only make you crazy. If they raise the subject, change it. If they persist, wave their questions aside with, "My advisor handles these things; finance does not interest me at all." Pick this moment to catch sight of a long-lost acquaintance well across the room, or bring up how the Celtics are doing this season.

Finally, there is one more psychological trick you can use to blunt the pain of bear markets, especially if you are a retiree who is drawing down his or her portfolio, and that is to occasionally relax your portfolio discipline a bit and think of your nest egg as consisting of two buckets: one filled with stocks and one filled with bonds. When stocks perform poorly, in order to raise living expenses you will be selling bonds, since their allocation will rise. Just do not forget to replenish the bond bucket with the proceeds of stock sales and to also take your living expenses from the stock bucket as well when times are flush.

Stop Making Analogies

Always remember: Poorly performing companies are usually good stocks, and vice versa. By the same token, unglamorous, slowly growing countries are often great markets; avoid making the classic mistake of conflating a rapidly growing economy with high equity returns.

This, of course, is just another variant of "dare to be dull." Our human desire to climb the pecking order by owning the most prestigious shoes, cars, and clothes applies equally well to the securities we own. You are definitely not going to impress your country club friends by telling them you own shares of Caterpillar Inc. or an index fund. Let them laugh; the joke is on them.

Relish the Randomness

As Gene Fama, the financial economist we met in Chapter 2, found out nearly a half century ago, almost all apparent stock market patterns are just a coincidence—the face of the man in the moon or the temporary image of the Empire State Building in the clouds scudding by. Do not even think about trying to extrapolate recent market moves into the future. The safest assumption you can make about changes in market price is that they are totally random, and while it is easy to come up with after-the-fact rationalizations of why stocks went up or down, always remember that no one consistently predicts bull and bear markets.

Recall too the stadium-full-of-coin-flippers analogy: Because so many professionals make predictions, a few will always be right at any one moment, purely by chance. It is just that their names change each year. Ignore them. Whenever I hear a market guru expounding on the radio or TV, I immediately picture them as one of Princeton professor Burton Malkiel's famous monkeys, throwing darts at a stock page.[20]

In order to combat these corrosive, pattern-seeking tendencies, I recommend two exercises. First, keep a log of your hunches for a while before you actually begin acting on them. After two or three years, review your predictions; the odds are overwhelming you will be glad you did not act on most of them. Never forget that the market is a mechanism designed to humiliate the maximum number of its participants.

Second, whenever it seems like recent good or bad stock or bond returns are going to continue forever, take a look at the longer-term data, and repeat over and over, "the long term is more important than the short run." Yes, for the 10 years ending in 2008, the S&P 500 has lost more than 1 percent per year even after reinvesting dividends; after taking inflation into account, this loss amounted to nearly 4 percent per year. Investors had every reason to be morose. But for the previous 10 years, 1989–1998, it returned over 19 percent per year. By the end of 1998, investors thought that we had entered a new era of permanently high stock returns.

A look at the longer-term data, and even more importantly, the Gordon Equation, reveals that neither the ebullient 1989–1998 decade nor the awful 1999–2008 decade was typical. The historical data show that between 1926 and 2008, the S&P 500 returned 9.62 percent, while the Gordon Equation suggests future returns that are slightly lower, in the 7–8 percent range (in nominal, before-inflation terms). As I have already said, while the Gordon Equation is likely a better predictor of future returns than even the longest-term historical data, both are far superior to the views in the rearview mirror in 1998 and 2008.

Finally, never forget legendary investor John Templeton's warning, that the four most expensive words in the English language are "This time it's different."

You Do Not Live in Lake Wobegon

In the investment world, you are not above average. You are likely not even close. Finance attracts the best and brightest in our society and then it gives them the best data and fastest computers. Whenever you buy or sell a stock or bond, you are competing against these well-endowed, well-equipped, workaholic pros; your odds of succeeding in this game are about the same as your chances of starting at third base for the Yankees next season.

Charles Ellis, one of investing's senior statesmen, puts it succinctly: There are only three ways to win the game. You can try to be smarter than everyone else. Trouble is, in this league you do not even come close. You can try to work harder than everyone else, but here, you do not stand a chance either, since many on Wall Street take no time off, and some do not sleep that much either. In Ellis's words,

> Watch a pro football game, and it's obvious the guys on the field are far faster, stronger, and more willing to bear and inflict pain than you are. Surely you would say, "I don't want to play against those guys!" Well, 90% of stock market volume is done by institutions, and half of that is done by the world's 50 largest investment firms, deeply committed, vastly well prepared—the smartest sons of bitches in the world working their tails off all day long. You know what? I don't want to play against those guys either.[21]

If Charley Ellis does not want to play that game, neither should you. However, according to Ellis there is a third way you *can* win, although this one is not easy either: the emotional one that amounts to buying and holding index funds for the long term (or at least buying when everyone else is a panicked mound of jelly, and selling when everyone else is ecstatically buying). But this amounts to not playing the game at all, which is the only way to play it.

I have one final admonition: Investors reading this book in 2009 will have little difficulty understanding the dangers of overestimating one's risk tolerance. But for those picking up this book in the 2010s or later, beware. Believing that you are risk tolerant and actually *being* risk tolerant are two entirely different things. It is easy to talk the talk; but walking the walk is an entirely different matter. If you have never been tested before, I strongly urge that you encounter your first bear market conservatively invested.

Mingle with the Masses

Want to join investing's real aristocracy? Become a federal employee and get access to the government's Thrift Savings Plan, whose funds charge an amazing 0.015 percent—you read that right, 1.5 basis points—in total fees and expenses.

By contrast, wealthy investors, and those trying to behave like them, are the cash cows of the financial services companies, and the not-so-complimentary name for them inside the industry is "whale." Do not become one. Avoid the lure of hedge funds, private investment pools, and exotic derivatives-based strategies. Buy fuddy-duddy, low-cost index funds. If it will make you feel any better, many index fund providers have a special share class with high minimums and ultra-low fees to keep out the great unwashed. Vanguard's Admiral Class shares, for example, typically charge only 0.09–0.20 percent in expenses, about half that charged by its ordinary Investor Class shares. Admiral Class shares require a $100,000 initial investment, versus only $3,000 for the Investor Class shares.

> Do not try to keep up with the investment Joneses; they have most likely just bought the Brooklyn Bridge.

Wake up, smell the coffee, and observe the private jets and eight-figure bonuses of brokerage executives, paid for by you, and the sub-par returns earned for you by these inept clowns. If you find yourself sitting, literally or figuratively, in a large, leather-and-mahogany-filled office across from someone who flies private from vacation house to vacation house, pivot 180 degrees and run like hell. As your father probably told you, when you cannot figure out who is the patsy at the poker table, then you are it.

Summary

- Beware glib, simple, narrative explanations of financial or economic events. There is no substitute for quantitatively estimating expected stock and bond returns as explained in Chapter 2.
- Eliminate excitement and novelty from your portfolio. Seeking them out can prove very expensive.
- Keep yourself in emotional shape by regularly rebalancing your portfolio, since this forces you to move in a direction opposite that of the crowd. The most important investment ability of all is emotional discipline.
- Beware analogies: Good companies are usually not good stocks; vigorously growing national economies often produce low returns.
- Do not see patterns where none exist; most of what happens in the financial markets in the short term is random noise.
- Regard yourself as average. When buying or selling a stock or bond, consider who you are trading against.
- Do not crave fancy investment vehicles; most will leave a sour taste. Plain-vanilla index funds will better nourish your retirement.

CHAPTER 5

Muggers and Worse

In the heady days of spring 2006, I spoke at a conference of wealth managers about the relationship between economic history and market returns. Before my talk, a tall, distinguished-looking advisor from a major Wall Street firm came over and introduced himself. Looking down at me—both literally and figuratively—he solemnly intoned, "Bernstein, for a doctor you write finance pretty well, but you just don't understand alternatives."

By alternatives, he meant the laundry list of then-popular, non-traditional investment products that his and other large investment firms peddled: commodities funds, structured investment vehicles, mortgage-backed securities, collateralized debt obligations, credit default swaps, auction-rate securities, and, above all, hedge funds.

All of these vehicles shared three characteristics: In the subsequent two years, a fair percent of them blew up; all of them charged high fees along the way; and all made the brokerage firms a lot of money. By not being skeptical enough about the motivations of the investment industry, millions of investors, and not a few supposedly sophisticated pension and endowment managers, lost trillions of dollars. The real tragedy was that this damage was entirely preventable.

The World's Largest Bad Neighborhood

In every city in this nation and in every town of any size, people avoid certain areas after dark. It is the same in the investment metropolis, with one slight variation: Here, you do not dare venture more than 10 yards from the front door.

The prudent investor treats almost the entirety of the financial industrial landscape as an urban combat zone. This means *any* stock broker or full-service brokerage firm, *any* newsletter, *any* advisor who purchases individual securities, *any* hedge fund. *Most* mutual fund companies spew more toxic waste into the investment environment than a third-world refinery. *Most* financial advisors cannot invest their way out a paper bag. Who can you trust? Almost no one.

Why this awful state of affairs in the investment industry? First and foremost, neither the industry nor the government impose any educational requirements on brokers or financial advisors, let alone the managers of hedge, pension, or mutual funds.

The level of financial knowledge of the average broker never ceases to appall me. Having gotten to this point in the book, you already know far more about finance than most of them. I have yet to meet a brokerage representative, for example, who has heard of Fama and French, knows the history of the securities markets in any detail, or can easily describe how risk levels affect investment returns over time.

Think about it: All doctors, lawyers, and accountants have the equivalent of post-graduate degrees and studied for years to pass grueling exams, yet your broker was not required to graduate high school. Worse, an incompetent or mendacious broker can devastate your net wealth much faster than even the least capable accountant. As frosting on the cake, he will get rich in the process.

> The average stock broker services his clients in the same way that Baby Face Nelson serviced banks.

Second, as I have already mentioned, people do not go into the financial services industry for the same reasons that attract individuals to social work, government service, or elementary education. It is rare to meet a hedge fund manager or mutual fund executive who has a vision of the world that extends very far beyond his or her own self-interest. It is not grossly unfair to observe that most seek employment at brokerage houses, hedge funds, and mutual funds for the same reason Willie Sutton supposedly offered for robbing banks: "Because that's where the money is." Consequently, you should extend an extra degree of caution to anyone who wants to manage your finances.

Third, and certainly not least, is what is known in economics as "agency conflict." Very simply, a mutual fund or brokerage company has two sets of masters: their mutual fund and brokerage clients, and the shareholders who own the stock of the brokerage or fund company itself. Every company's goal is to maximize the bottom line of the latter—its real owners—and mutual fund and brokerage firms can only do this at the expense of their clients. In practice, the company's primary goal is to bleed its clients as copiously as possible to feed its shareholders and management.

Should not the best interest of the mutual fund or brokerage firm be to treat its clients well in order to retain their business? No. From the clients' perspective, the best practice is to purchase index funds, and it is not difficult to acquire them for 0.10–0.20 percent in annual fees. On the other hand, mutual fund families can easily convince gullible investors to buy the "superior performance" of an actively managed fund that on average will lose 2 percent per year to fees and transactional expenses. A broker will have little difficulty extracting the same amount in commissions and from other more opaque revenue sources every year. Even if the brokerage client or active fund owner figures this out and leaves after a year or two, the firm has already made more money than an ethical outfit would in decades; if the client never figures it out, and most never do, so much the better. In the investment industry, honesty is most definitely not the best policy.

One hoary investment company story describes a young broker asking an old one about the secret to his success. The latter replies, "It's simple; over the years I've slowly transferred my client's assets to my own name."

This is no joke. Assume that a client of the old broker started out in January 1969 with $1,000; further assume that each year the broker extracted 3 percent in fees from that portfolio and invested it in his own account. Last, assume that the broker and client both invested in the S&P 500. The client received each year's S&P 500 return minus the 3 percent fees and commissions, and the broker invested in an index fund (as many do) with 0.20 percent expenses. Figure 5.1 shows what actually happens in this situation: By 1993, the broker now has a larger account than the client, and by the end of 2008, he has accumulated more than twice as much in assets!

It turns out that stock brokers are very highly trained—just not in finance. Their employers teach them very well indeed the art of the soft sell. One journalist, who went undercover at Merrill Lynch and Prudential-Bache, found that most trainees had no financial background at all; as one of them, a used car salesman, wryly put it, "Investments were just another vehicle." Both financial companies did school their charges in the basics of stocks and bonds, but only enough to give clients the impression that they knew what they were selling.

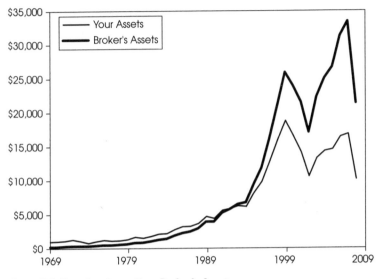

Figure 5.1 Your Assets vs. Your Broker's Assets

The bulk of the training observed by the reporter centered in language-lab-type facilities, where the neophytes endlessly rehearsed and discussed sophisticated sales scripts. The brokerage firms specifically designed these well-oiled spiels to draw from clients their needs and fears. Fifty years ago, "IBM is about to take off, and I'd like to put you into 300 shares right now" served very well for Ozzie Nelson. In more recent decades, "What do you worry about most, Mrs. Johnson?" produces more sales. After completing their training, one of the companies encouraged their graduates to get their real estate and insurance licenses and make a minimum of 180 cold calls per day.[1]

Almost no objective data exist on the behavior and performance of broker-run accounts. Do you want to know what the turnover, total expenses, or return of your portfolio were? You are likely to be out of luck. Even more remarkably, neither the SEC nor the brokerage industry's self-regulatory agency, the Financial Industry Regulatory Authority (FINRA), who are both charged with looking after the public interest, maintain data on how brokers actually invest and on how well they actually perform.

What little we do know comes from everyday observation of the industry. Rarely do brokers recommend the purchase of Treasury securities or index funds, since they produce scant commission revenue. Far more common are the sales of individual corporate and municipal bonds that carry enormous profit margins. Typically, these are "principal transactions," in which the brokerage firm buys and sells the bonds out of its own inventory. The broker usually tells the client that "there was no commission," as if he or she has just been given a Christmas gift.

What the broker has not told the client is that the firm had very likely just bought the bond from another of its customers for several percent less than the price it sold it to him or her. Since, at least until very recently, daily quotes of individual municipal and bond transactions were not easily available, both buyers and sellers remained ignorant of how badly they were being fleeced.

Another well-hidden abuse is the "special": stocks and bonds underwritten by the firm's investment banking division and rejected by savvier institutional investors. Generally, the firm will disburse nights out on the town, exotic vacations, and occasionally even expensive automobiles to brokers who unload the largest amounts of this rubbish on their unsuspecting clients. Obviously, the brokerage houses do not advertise this activity, but it is not unusual for outside advisors to find brokerage accounts larded with obscure newly issued stocks and bonds that have "special" written all over them.

Clients engage brokers with the expectation that they will provide them with market-beating security recommendations. It would be nice if their stock and bond picks resulted from careful research and analysis, but, alas, they are experts in sales, not security selection. (If they were any good at the latter, they certainly would not have become mere brokers.) More likely, their recommendations came over the "squawk box," a communications system linking headquarters with dozens, hundreds, or even thousands of offices. Several times per day, the squawk box blares with the firm's analysts' latest stock and bond picks.

These recommendations are not entirely worthless, but it would be better if the retail client was not getting sloppy seconds, for it is almost certain that this information has been first given to the company's institutional clients, mutual funds, and privately managed, wealthy clients. By the time word reaches the small investor, the price of the stock has been bid up and any advantage is lost.

Conflict of interest with the firm's investment banking division seriously erodes the integrity of the analyst recommendations; if he or she angers a company with a harsh opinion of its stock, that company is unlikely to favor the brokerage's investment banking arm with the next new stock or bond issue. Analysts have little problem with the words "outperform," "accumulate," and "hold," but their vocabularies seem to lack the word "sell."

Things got especially out of hand in the late 1990s as the dot-com initial public offering (IPO) market yielded enormous investment banking profits. Tech analysts such as Mary Meeker and Henry Blodget shamelessly touted stocks with the aim of garnering business for their firms, and investors found out too late on which side the analysts' bread was being buttered. (In fairness, after settling a fraud case brought by the SEC, Mr. Blodget realized the error of his ways and has become a strong critic of the industry and an advocate of passive and indexed investing. A talented interviewer and writer, he has become a frequent contributor to *Slate* and *Newsweek*.)

If you feel compelled to read analyst reports, make sure they come from an independent research firm that has no investment banking affiliation. Alas, small investors do not usually have access to such outfits, which generally sell their services for astronomical prices to large institutions.

The question remaining is: Why isn't the public as well protected from malfeasance in the brokerage industry as it is in, for example, medicine, dentistry, accounting, and law? The reason is that all four of these professions are highly regulated, and their practitioners deviate from standard procedure only at great peril to their livelihood. If a physician fails to recognize and treat with powerful antibiotics more than one or two cases of obvious bacterial pneumonia, his license will get yanked with gusto. Ditto for the accountant or attorney who regularly falls below the standard of practice.

The same is not true for brokers. The depressing fact of the matter is that federal and state governments do not regulate brokers in the same way they do other professionals. For example, the law does not consider brokers to be fiduciaries, as are practitioners of other learned professions. This arcane term refers to a professional's duty to put a client's interests first. Accountants, lawyers, bankers, and doctors all have fiduciary responsibility to clients and patients, as do investment advisors.

Somehow, the brokerage industry dodged this bullet. It adds insult to injury that in few other businesses are the interests of the client so divergent from that of the practitioner; every penny in fees and commissions paid by the client goes directly to the broker's bottom line.*

---

*As this book is going to press, the Obama administration has proposed a sweeping overhaul of financial regulation that includes applying fiduciary standards to the brokerage industry.

Unlike your doctor, lawyer, or accountant, your broker is not a fiduciary: that is, he is under no legal obligation to place your interests above his own.

In some respects, this state of affairs is a historical accident. All the professions I have mentioned, except brokerage, have long since recognized that the regulation of minimal standards of training and practice is a necessity. A century ago, it happened to the medical profession with the publication of the Flexner Report. Bluntly put, there is no chance that your doctor, dentist, or attorney is a high-school dropout. Your stockbroker, however, just might be.

The Fund Funhouse

The message of the preceding pages could not be clearer: Do not come anywhere near a stock broker or a brokerage firm; sooner rather than later, you will get fleeced. Further, since they owe you no fiduciary duty, you will have little legal protection absent outright fraud or the sale of an outrageously unsuitable investment.

The terrain presented by the mutual fund industry is only slightly less hostile, but because it features greater transparency and the protections offered by the Investment Company Act of 1940, it gives you at least a fighting chance of emerging with your wealth intact.

Let's start by listing the advantages of mutual funds.

- Wide diversification: Most mutual funds own hundreds of securities, largely protecting you against the blowup of a single stock. Of course, this is not a slam-dunk, as demonstrated in Chapter 2 by poor Mr. Miller, a "superstar" manager who held a relatively small number of companies.

- Transparency of expenses: Unlike brokers, fund companies publish their fees and expenses in fund prospectuses and regular reports. They do not publish their transactional costs, but these can be estimated by looking at the level of turnover, the size of the fund, and the size of the companies they own, all of which are available. Since stock mutual funds lose about 0.1 percent of return for every 10 percent of turnover, the lower the turnover, the better.
- Professional management: While your broker might be a former used car salesman, your fund manager very likely has an advanced degree in finance or economics and is more than familiar with the fundamental principles described in this book. This will almost certainly not enable him to beat the market over the long haul, but his education and training make him less likely to commit the sorts of simple but disastrous errors so regularly perpetrated by brokers.
- Protection: The Investment Company Act of 1940 provides a highly effective barrier between the fund company and your assets. Outright fraud involving a mutual fund company is vanishingly rare, as opposed to brokerage fraud, which is not.
- Ease of execution: With a few mouse clicks, you can obtain the sort of portfolio diversification your parents could only dream of.

So far, so good. Unfortunately, the diversification, transparency, expertise, protection, and convenience of the modern fund company do not eliminate two of the three biggest problems plaguing the financial services industry as a whole: the Willie Sutton phenomenon and agency conflict.

Few brokers resemble Albert Schweitzer or Mother Teresa, and the same is true of mutual fund managers and fund company executives. Similar to the brokerage industry, they owe their primary allegiance not to the fund's share-holders—that is you, the investor—but rather to the company's shareholders. As put so well by the great economist Paul Samuelson:

> I decided there was only one place to make money in the mutual fund business as there is only one place for a temperate man to be in a saloon, behind the bar and not in front of it . . . so I invested in a management company.[2]

Simply put, since mutual fund company revenues flow proportionately from assets under management (AUM), they focus primarily on growing the size of their funds, and not on your returns. The good news is that the link between AUM and performance is far tighter than it is with a brokerage account. Mutual funds present less opportunity for monkey business, since they regularly report performance and fees and you can so easily move assets from a stock fund to a money market fund, from which you can write a personal check.

That said, a wide gap still separates the interests of the investors in funds from those of the fund companies. I know of no better precis of this conflict of interest than a speech given by Jason Zweig to the Investment Company Institute in 1997, where he drew the distinction between an "investment company," a mutual fund firm whose operations favor the fund shareholders, and a "marketing company," a mutual fund firm whose operations favor the company's owners. Here is how Mr. Zweig tells the difference:

> Marketing firms create large numbers of fledgling "incubator funds." Purely by chance, a few will perform spectacularly. The firm then advertises the bejabbers out of this randomly high performance and attracts

assets from the gullible. Investment companies do not do this.

As AUM increases, the fund benefits from increasing economy of scale. Marketing firms do not pass these per-share savings on to the fund holders by dropping their fees, but rather direct the savings to their bottom lines. Investment companies pass these savings to the fund shareholders with fee reductions.

Marketing firms cherry pick their best funds over the most favorable time periods, producing "mountain charts as steep as the Alps" in their advertising. Investment companies do not.

Marketing firms pay their fund managers according to AUM, not performance. Investment companies do not.

Marketing firms do not educate their clients about investment risks, particularly during long bull markets. The investment company repeatedly does so.[3]

In addition, marketing firms have a nasty habit of self-dealing in their security transactions. Mutual funds pay an enormous amount in commissions and spreads to the brokerage firms that buy and sell securities for their funds. Too often, the fund companies cannot resist the temptation to take kickbacks from the brokerage companies in return for excessive commissions (usually in the form of so-called "soft dollars") or, worse, to direct trades to their own affiliated brokerage arm. Mutual fund investors are almost always unaware of the existence of such shady deals and of how much of their wealth they siphon off.

Unfortunately, unless you are an expert in the field, you will not have access to this sort of information. To make it simple: The ownership structure of any financial services company ultimately determines just how well it serves its shareholders in the long run. Table 5.1 demonstrates this vividly; out of 18 large fund families, the "nonprofit" and privately owned ones are ranked first, second, third, sixth, and ninth, with fund companies owned by publicly traded parent firms bringing up the rear.

> Do not invest with any mutual fund family that is owned by a publicly traded parent company.

Table 5.1 Mutual Fund Performance and Ownership Structure

Rank	Company	Ownership Structure	% of Funds with 4–5 Morningstar Stars	% of Funds with 1–2 Morningstar Stars
1.	Vanguard	Mutual	59%	5%
2.	DFA	Private	57%	7%
3.	TIAA-CREF	Nonprofit	54%	4%
4.	T Rowe Price	Publicly Traded	53%	9%
5.	Janus	Publicly Traded	54%	16%
6.	American	Private	46%	20%
7.	Franklin Temp.	Publicly Traded	31%	22%
8.	Morgan Stanley	Publicly Traded	32%	30%
9.	Fidelity	Private	31%	34%
10.	Barclays	Publicly Traded	27%	31%
11.	AIM Invest	Publicly Traded	20%	34%
12.	Columbia	Publicly Traded	23%	38%
13.	Goldman Sachs	Publicly Traded	15%	55%
14.	Dreyfus	Publicly Traded	12%	53%
15.	MainStay	Publicly Traded	20%	60%
16.	John Hancock	Publicly Traded	17%	60%
17.	ING	Publicly Traded	9%	64%
18.	Putnam	Publicly Traded	4%	62%

Note: the ranking is the combined scoring obtained from the percent of funds with 4–5 stars, and the inverse of the number of funds with 1–2 stars.

Source: John C. Bogle, "A New Order of Things—Bringing Mutuality to the 'Mutual' Fund," speech given at George Washington University Law School, February 19, 2008. Courtesy of John C. Bogle.

This is no accident. In today's hypervigilant markets, the fund company's attention is focused laser-like on next quarter's corporate earnings. Remember, we are talking here about the profits of the fund companies themselves, *not* the investment returns to the companies' mutual fund shareholders, who are their customers.

Sooner rather than later, the publicly traded fund companies' profits must be paid for by its customers: you, the milch cows of the industry.

In the best of all possible worlds, the fund company has no publicly or privately owned shares and is instead held directly by the mutual fund shareholders. As we discussed in Chapter 2, only one fund company does this: the Vanguard Group. Its domestic stock index funds generally charge between 0.09 and 0.30 percent, and its actively managed and foreign funds a tad more. By contrast, the average actively managed domestic stock fund charges 1.35 percent per year, and the average foreign fund even more.

Next on the list are privately run firms, the largest being Fidelity Investments, Dimensional Fund Advisors, and the American Funds. The key point about these companies is that their shares do not trade publicly, and thus they do not have to publicly report their earnings every quarter. While these for-profit entities are certainly not immune to agency conflict, they tend to have a longer-term focus that benefits their customers, the shareholders of their mutual funds. Let's treat each in turn.

Fidelity Investments is owned and largely run by the Johnson family. The firm was founded by Edward C. Johnson II in 1949 and later passed to his capable and forward-looking son, Edward C. "Ned" Johnson III, who brought the company into the computer age earlier and more forcefully than the competition. Ned also was possessed of a special genius for providing the investing public with the hottest "flavor of the month" funds. You say that

Brazilian bonds or wind technology is hot right now? Then Ned has a fund for you.

By Mr. Zweig's definition, Fidelity is most definitely a marketing company, but one with two saving graces. First, its family ownership structure encourages a more client-oriented culture aimed at retaining its shareholder base. This means slightly lower fees than those of other fund families. Second, and more importantly, Fidelity offers very low-priced, passively managed funds. They are so low-priced, in fact, that they serve as loss leaders, designed to get you into the store to buy its more expensive funds. As long as you keep to the discount rack, you should do well there.

The American Funds group is even more of an oddity. Owned by Capital Group Companies, a privately held concern, they provide funds to advisors and brokers that carry "load fees" of various sorts in order to compensate them, and of course to fleece you. In spite of this, their investment culture is among the most disciplined and focused in the business, and their long-term track record is not bad. Were someone to force me to purchase an actively managed load fund, I would buy one from American Funds. (In certain situations, investors can purchase their funds without loads.)

In 1981, David Booth and Rex Sinquefield cofounded Dimensional Fund Advisors, which we have already briefly mentioned. Its spiritual father is none other than Eugene Fama, originator of the efficient market hypothesis. Ken French, Fama's major collaborator throughout the years, designs the funds; all are passively managed, and most are heavily weighted to small and/or value stocks. The company is privately owned, mainly by Booth and Sinquefield, and Fama and French both maintain an active presence there. Because of the private ownership structure, their fund fees are perhaps by 0.10 to 0.20 percent per year higher than those that Vanguard might charge if they offered the same asset classes (which they do not). If you are looking for value and small exposure, this is the place to go.

The only problem with Dimensional is that you will need to pay an advisor to gain access to them. In my opinion, if you are capable of managing your own investments, it is not worth the advisor fee, which can run from 0.5 to 2 percent per year. However, if you are going to hire an advisor, make sure he or she has access to, and uses, Dimensional's products.

Finally, there is one publicly traded company that I can recommend with some trepidation, and that is Barclays, whose iShares series of exchange-traded funds (ETFs) are the leaders in this field. I am not wild about ETFs, but they do offer small investors indexed products in more esoteric asset classes that are not covered by Vanguard and Fidelity. As this is being written, unfortunately, iShares has just been purchased by BlackRock, thus clouding its future.

Summary

- You are engaged in a life-and-death struggle with the financial services industry. Every dollar in fees, expenses, and spreads you pay them comes directly out of your pocket. If you act on the assumption that every broker, insurance salesman, mutual fund salesperson, and financial advisor you encounter is a hardened criminal, you will do just fine.

- Both mutual fund companies and brokerage houses know more ways than you can count of fleecing you without your knowing it.

- Invest, if you can, only with nonprofit mutual fund companies. If you must work with profit-making entities, they should be privately owned. If forced to work with a financial services company that belongs to a publicly traded parent, buy only those products that come with the lowest expenses and turnover; this usually means exchange-traded funds.

CHAPTER 6

Building Your Portfolio

How much money will you need in retirement? How much should you save to get there? Once you have retired, how much of your portfolio should you spend in retirement? The answers to these questions boil down to two simple rules: First, save as much as you can, start as early as you can, and do not ever stop. Second, consider an immediate fixed annuity in retirement.

Financial Planning for a Lifetime: The Basics

Each dollar you do not save at 25 will mean two inflation-adjusted dollars that you will need to save if you start at age 35, four if you begin at 45, and eight if you start at 55. In practice, if you lack substantial savings at 45, you are in serious trouble. Since a 25-year-old should be saving at least 10 percent of his or her salary, this means that a 45-year-old will need to save nearly half of his or her salary. Most 45-year-olds will find this nearly impossible, if for no other reason than the necessity of paying living expenses, payroll taxes, and income taxes.

Some retirement experts have argued that such aggressive over-saving risks "under-consuming" during an investor's prime years—that is, unnecessarily depriving yourself now in order to be perfectly safe in the future. I respectfully disagree, and urge you to remember Pascal's Wager. The possible adverse consequences of under-consuming in your youth or middle age pale in comparison to the risks of not saving enough for old age.

If you hope to avoid outliving your money, you may very well have to spend some of your nest egg to purchase an immediate fixed annuity when you retire. These vehicles, sold by insurance companies, provide a fixed monthly payment until death; spouses can be covered at extra cost.

True, by purchasing an annuity, you "lose control" of your money and in most circumstances there will be nothing left for your heirs. However, if you do not annuitize, it is depressing to realize just how little of your nest egg you will be able to safely spend. As far as your heirs are concerned, ensuring that you will not become a financial burden to them should more than offset the smaller inheritance.

My rule of thumb is that if you spend 2 percent of your nest egg per year, adjusted upward for the cost of living, you are as secure as possible; at 3 percent, you are probably safe; at 4 percent, you are taking real risks; and at 5 percent, you had better like cat food and vacations very close to home. For example, if, in addition to Social Security and pensions, you spend $50,000 per year in living expenses, that means you will need $2.5 million to be perfectly safe, and $1.67 million to be fairly secure. If you have "only" $1.25 million, you are taking chances; if you are starting with $1 million, there is a good chance you will eventually run out of money.

By contrast, it is possible to find immediate fixed annuities yielding a 6 to 8 percent inflation-adjusted payout (depending upon your age at purchase, your gender, and your survivorship benefits). The higher payout comes from the few percent of your fellow annuitants who die each year, diverting their payout stream in your direction. In other words, you are pooling your mortality risk with others, and by doing so insure yourself against living too long. If you survive to a ripe old age, you will benefit from the capital of those who did not. The best annuity deal available, paradoxically, comes to you courtesy of Uncle Sam: deferring Social Security until age 70. Waiting until 70 increases by almost one-third the monthly payment you would get starting at age 66. Conversely, starting at 62 reduces the payment you would have gotten at 66 by over a quarter. This calculates out to a guaranteed real return from waiting of 8 percent per year, which is hard to beat anywhere in the capital markets. Should you "live too long," the bigger monthly check will come in very handy indeed.

Unless you are very fortunate, you will likely not have saved sufficient assets to last into a ripe old age. Most retirees should purchase "longevity insurance" by postponing Social Security until age 70, and perhaps by adding a commercial immediate fixed annuity as well.

For many retirees, delaying Social Security until age 70 will not reduce the amount that they have to withdraw from their nest egg to the safe 2–4 percent per year spending rate; in that case, they should consider purchasing additional annuity income from an insurance company. The problems and pitfalls of doing so will be discussed later in the chapter.

Saving for Retirement: Nuts and Bolts

What does the asset allocation process look like while you are saving? Which vehicles should you use? What should your allocation look like before and after retirement?

Chapter 2 described several possible portfolios. Recall that we began with an overall stock/bond allocation pegged to your age and risk tolerance, and then further allocated the stock assets according to the size of the portfolio and your tolerance for complexity.

Tables 6.1, 6.2, and 6.3, respectively, summarize my recommendations for executing these allocations with domestic stock, foreign stock, and bond mutual funds. For each asset class, I have listed traditional open-end funds, which can be bought or sold only once per day, at the 4 P.M. Eastern closing market price.

Note also that many of the Vanguard funds are available in three share classes: Investor-Class shares that carry a $3,000 minimum; Admiral-Class shares that have much lower fees consonant with their $100,000 minimum ($50,000 if you have held the fund for more than 10 years); and exchange-traded funds (ETFs) that carry slightly lower fees than the Admiral-Class shares.

ETF offerings are listed in the notes at the bottoms of the tables. These are essentially the same as mutual funds, except that they trade on stock exchanges and can be bought and sold throughout market hours. In addition, because of the way these shares are created and redeemed, they can be somewhat more tax-efficient than traditional, open-end mutual fund shares. These advantages come at a cost, since trading them incurs commissions and buy-sell spreads.

I have nothing against ETFs, but I do believe that most investors are better served by the more traditional open-end mutual funds for three reasons. First, the commission and spread costs incurred by ETFs will quickly erode their minuscule expense advantage. As you can see from Tables 6.1 and 6.2, in several cases the ETFs are actually more expensive than the corresponding Vanguard or Fidelity funds. Second, I see the supposed convenience of being able to trade ETFs throughout the day as a psychological disadvantage. Unless you are able to predict intraday market moves—a fool's errand if ever there was one—you are faced with the oftentimes paralyzing choice of exactly when to buy or sell. Better to accept the end-of-day pricing of a traditional open-end fund and be done with it. Finally, I believe that the institutional risks of ETFs are considerable. To be blunt, I do

Table 6.1 Low-Cost Domestic Equity Mutual Funds

Fund	Index	Type	Symbol	Expense Ratio	Minimum Reg./IRA	Taxable/ Sheltered
Large-Cap Market						
Vanguard 500 Index	S&P 500	Open-end	VFINX	0.18%**	$3,000	Both
Vanguard Tax-Managed Growth & Income	S&P 500	Open-end	VTGIX	0.21%*	$3,000	Taxable
Vanguard Tax-Managed Capital Appreciation	Russell 1000	Open-end	VMCAX	0.21%*	$10,000	Taxable
Vanguard Large-Cap Index	MSCI 750	Open-end	VLACX	0.26%**	$3,000	Both
Fidelity Spartan 500 Index	S&P 500	Open-end	FSMKX	0.10%	$10,000	Both
iShares S&P 500 Index	S&P 500	ETF	IVV	0.09%	None	Both
SPDRs	S&P 500	ETF	SPY	0.08%	None	Both
Vanguard Total Stock Market	Wilshire 5000	Open-end	VTSMX	0.18%**	$3,000	Both
Fidelity Spartan Total Stock Market	Wilshire 5000	Open-end	FSTMX	0.10%	$10,000	Both
iShares Total Stock Market	Dow Jones Total Stock Mkt.	ETF	IYY	0.20%	None	Both
Small-Cap Market						
Vanguard Small Cap Index	Russell 2000	Open-end	NAESX	0.28%**	$3,000	Sheltered
Vanguard Tax-Managed Small Cap Index	S&P 600	Open-end	VTMSX	0.19%*	$10,000	Taxable
iShares S&P 600 Small-Cap Index	S&P 600	ETF	IJR	0.20%	None	Sheltered
iShares Russell 2000 Index	Russell 2000	ETF	IWM	0.20%	None	Sheltered

(Continued)

Table 6.1 (*Continued*)

Fund	Index	Type	Symbol	Expense Ratio	Minimum Reg./IRA	Taxable/ Sheltered
Large-Cap Value						
Vanguard Value Index	MSCI Prime Barra Value	Open-end	VIVAX	0.26%**	$3,000	Sheltered
iShares Russell 1000 Value Index	Russell 1000	ETF	IWD	0.20%	None	Sheltered
iShares S&P 500/ Barra Value Index	S&P 500/ Barra Value	ETF	IVE	0.18%	None	Sheltered
Small-Cap Value						
Vanguard Small- Cap Value Index	MSCI U.S. Small-Cap Value	Open-end	VISVX	0.28%***	$3,000	Sheltered
iShares Russell 2000 Value Index	Russell 2000 Value	ETF	IWN	0.25%	None	Sheltered
iShares S&P SC 600 Value Index	S&P 600- SCBarra Value	ETF	IJS	0.25%	None	Sheltered
REIT						
Vanguard REIT Index	MSCI REIT	Open-end	VGSIX	0.26%****	$3,000	Sheltered
iShares REIT	Dow Jones REIT	ETF	IYR	0.48%	None	Sheltered

* One percent redemption fee for shares held less than five years. Admiral-Class and ETF shares not available.

** Also available as Admiral-Class shares and ETFs.

*** Also available as ETFs. Admiral Class not available.

**** One percent redemption fee for shares held less than one year; Admiral Class and ETF available.

Source: The Vanguard Group and www.morningstar.com.

not trust most of the ETF providers to support these products over the very long term; all except Vanguard are publicly traded entities. As this is being written, for example, the largest ETF family, Barclays iShares, seems to have been sold to BlackRock Inc., a huge publicly traded financial services

Table 6.2 Low-Cost International Equity Mutual Funds

Fund	Index	Type	Symbol	Expense Ratio	Minimum Reg./IRA	Taxable/ Sheltered
Vanguard Total International	EAFE	Open-end	VGTSX	0.39%***	$3,000	Sheltered
Vanguard Developed Markets	EAFE–EM	Open-end	VDMIX	0.29%***	$3,000	Both
Vanguard Tax-Managed International	N/A	Open-end	VTMGX	0.20%*	$3,000	Taxable
Vanguard European	EAFE–E	Open-end/ ETF	VEURX	0.29%**	$3,000	Both
Vanguard Pacific	EAFE–P	Open-end/ ETF	VPACX	0.29%**	$3,000	Both
Vanguard Emerging Markets	EAFE–EM	Open-end/ ETF	VEIEX	0.39%*****	$3,000	Both
Vanguard All-World ex-U.S. Small Cap	FTSE All-World ex-U.S.	Open-end/ ETF	VFSVX	0.60%****	$3,000	Sheltered
Fidelity Spartan International	EAFE	Open-end	FSIIX	0.10%	$10,000	Both
iShares MSCI Value	EAFE–Value	ETF	EFV	0.40%	None	Both
iShares Global Real Estate ex-U.S.	FTSE EPRA/ NAREIT Global RE ex-U.S.	ETF	IFGL	0.48%	None	Sheltered

* One percent redemption fee for shares held less than five years. Admiral-Class and ETF shares not available.

** Two percent redemption fee for shares held less than two months. Also available as Admiral-Class shares and as ETFs.

*** Two percent redemption fee for shares held less than two months.

**** Three-fourths percent purchase and sales; ETF; Admiral Class not available. ETF shares preferred because of lower expense.

***** 0.25% Purchase and Redemption Fees, also available in Admiral Class and as ETF.

Source: The Vanguard Group and www.morningstar.com.

Table 6.3 Low-Cost Bond Funds

Fund	Index	Average Duration/ Maturity (Years, as of 1/31/09)	Symbol	Expense Ratio	Minimum Reg./IRA	Taxable/ Sheltered
Vanguard Total Bond Index	Lehman/ Barclays Aggregate	3.7/5.4	VBMFX	0.22%*	$3,000	Both
Vanguard Short-Term Bond Index	Lehman/ Barclays 1–5 Yr. Govt./Credit	2.6/2.8	VBISX	0.22%*	$3,000	Both
Vanguard Short-Term Investment Grade	N/A	2.1/2.6	VFSTX	0.26%**	$3,000	Both
Vanguard Short-Term Treasury	N/A	2.4/2.7	VFISX	0.22%**	$3,000	Both
Vanguard Short-Term Tax-Exempt	N/A	1.1/1.3	VWSTX	0.20%**	$3,000	Taxable
Vanguard Limited-Term Tax-Exempt	N/A	2.6/2.7	VMTLX	0.20%**	$3,000	Taxable
Vanguard Int-Term Tax-Exempt	N/A	5.9/7.3	VWITX	0.20%**	$3,000	Taxable
Vanguard California Int.-Term Tax-Exempt	N/A	6.1/7.6	VCAIX	0.20%**	$3,000	Taxable
Vanguard Florida. Long-Term Tax-Exempt	N/A	7.5/13.1	VFLTX	0.20%**	$3,000	Taxable
Vanguard Mass. Long-Term Tax-Exempt	N/A	7.0/10.5	VMATX	0.17%	$3,000	Taxable

(Continued)

Table 6.3 (Continued)

Fund	Index	Average Duration/ Maturity (Years, as of 1/31/09)	Symbol	Expense Ratio	Minimum Reg./IRA	Taxable/ Sheltered
Vanguard New Jersey Long-Term Tax-Exempt	N/A	6.7/9.8	VNJTX	0.20%**	$3,000	Taxable
Vanguard New York Long-Term Tax-Exempt	N/A	7.6/12.7	VNYTX	0.20%**	$3,000	Taxable
Vanguard Ohio Long-Term Tax-Exempt	N/A	7.1/12.3	VOHIX	0.17%	$3,000	Taxable
Vanguard Pennsylvania Long-Term Tax-Exempt	N/A	6.7/10.1	VPAIX	0.20%**	$3,000	Taxable
Vanguard High-Yield Corporate	N/A	4.0/6.2	VWEHX	0.32%***	$3,000	Sheltered
Vanguard Inflation-Protected Securities	N/A	5.8/8.8	VIPSX	0.25%**	$3,000	Sheltered

* Available as Admiral Class and ETF.

** Available as Admiral Class.

*** One percent redemption fee for shares held less than one year. Available as Admiral-Class shares.

Source: The Vanguard Group and www.morningstar.com.

company—not a reassuring turn of events. If you must buy an ETF, then one from Vanguard, which is much more likely to be around in a generation than the other companies offering these products, should be your first choice.

That said, I think that there are a few instances in which an ETF does make sense. The first is the iShares EAFE (international) value ETF, for which Vanguard offers no corresponding index/passive mutual fund. The second is the Vanguard All-World ex-U.S. Small-Cap ETF, which does not charge the 0.75 percent purchase fee levied on the investor-class shares and also carries a much lower expense ratio (0.38 versus 0.60 percent). The third would be the iShares inter-national REIT fund (IFGL), for which there is no equivalent open-end fund available to most small investors.

How to Save: Dollar Cost Averaging and Value Averaging

Let's assume that you are relatively young and are still actively saving a significant portion of your salary. Just how does your savings plan mesh with your asset allocation policy?

We will start with the traditional and venerable way of doing so: dollar cost averaging (DCA), where a fixed dollar amount is periodically invested in stocks and bonds.

To see how this works, assume that you have decided on a 67/33 stock/bond portfolio consisting of equal parts of a U.S. total stock market index fund, an international stock index fund, and a total bond market index fund (that is, two-thirds stocks, one-third bonds).

Let's further assume that you are saving $300 per month, with $100 going into each fund, and that one of the stock funds, the international one, is extremely volatile, fluc-tuating in price between $5, $10, and $15 per share. If three successive purchases of $100 are made each month, here is what happens:

	Purchase	Price	Shares Bought
Month 1	$100	$15	6.67
Month 2	$100	$5	20.00
Month 3	$100	$10	10.00
Total	$300		36.67
Average Price per Share	$8.18		

Since more shares were bought at the lowest price, $5, the average price paid per share, $8.18, is actually lower than the average price for the three months, $10. DCA forces investors, if they have the fortitude, to invest equal amounts periodically. It lowers the average price paid for their purchases and thus increases their overall returns.

> Young savers should adhere to a disciplined savings plan using the dollar cost averaging or value averaging techniques.

Of course, this is an extreme example; even in the most volatile of markets, you will almost never see this sort of fluctuation within three successive months with any of these asset classes. But the point remains the same: DCA forces investors to purchase more shares at low prices than at high ones, increasing overall long-term returns.

There is an even better way to apply this buy-low discipline. Harvard finance professor Michael Edleson pioneered a technique called "value averaging," involving the methodical building up of individual stock and bond positions according to a precise mathematical formula.[1] This method is the most powerful tool I know of for gradually deploying retirement savings.

The technique works this way. In its most simplified version, target amounts would be established for each fund as follows:

	U.S. Total Stock	International Stock	Total Bond
Month 1	$100	$100	$100
Month 2	$200	$200	$200
Month 3	$300	$300	$300
Month 4	$400	$400	$400

At first blush, this looks as if it accomplishes the same thing as the previous DCA example, where $100 is simply added to each fund each month.

But it is not the same process at all. The amounts in the table are *targets*. For example, this means that if the U.S. Large-Cap fund started Month 3 with $300 in assets, and then fell 10 percent in value over the next 30 days to $270, our saver would have to add $130, not $100, to top it off to $400 at the start of Month 4. Conversely, if international stocks rose by 10 percent to $330 in value, then only $70 must be added.

This technique buys even more shares at lower prices and fewer at higher prices than with DCA and further boosts long-term returns. This does not come for free, of course: It requires more discipline than DCA, which itself is no walk in the park during a prolonged bear market. For those who are interested in the technique, I strongly recommend reading *Value Averaging*, in which Professor Edleson lays out its nuances, mainly having to do with where to get the money for the higher purchases during bear markets and how to adjust for the long-term tendency for stock prices to rise.

Four Investors, Four Plans

Four characters from an earlier book proved to be such a hit that I am going to call them back into service to illustrate how the process works in various age groups and tax situations: Young Yvonne, Sheltered Sam, Taxable Ted, and In-Between Ida.[2]

Young Yvonne (No Assets, Just Starting to Save)

Of all investors, young ones face the largest hurdles. Not only do they find it nearly impossible to contemplate the need to save for their own far-distant retirements, but even if they do, our inexorably materialist culture bombards them with a constant stream of toxic consumerist claptrap that obliterates the ability to save.

Luckily, Yvonne seems to have evaded this scourge. A tough childhood forged both her personal and financial character: After her father ran off during her teens, she was left to care for her two younger siblings and her mother, who fell into a miasma of drug abuse and a string of increasingly violent boyfriends.

Through a combination of scholarship money, frugality, and incredibly hard work, she eventually earned a night-school law degree and passed the bar exam on her first try. She has just started working as a public defender, and things are looking up: After she pays for her groceries, rent, and the upkeep on her 20-year-old Honda Civic, she has $3,000 left to put in her 401(k), which her employer matches dollar for dollar, for total annual retirement savings of $6,000.

Yvonne has recently seen too many of her friends lose their jobs, and this has convinced her that accumulating a 6-month emergency fund should be her first priority. On the other hand, she doesn't want to lose her employer match, which is essentially "free money," so for the next year she has resolved to forego vacations and to severely limit movie nights and eating out so that she can fund both her emergency fund and her 401(k) account.

Let's begin with Yvonne's allocation. For starters, she is a market virgin. So no matter how risk-tolerant she *thinks* she is, she should limit her stock/bond mix to 50/50. To keep things simple, she will begin with just three asset classes: a U.S. total stock market fund, an international stock fund, and a short-term bond fund.

We have not talked much thus far about asset allocation among bond asset classes. The general rule here is "keep it short, and keep it high quality." The bond portion of the portfolio serves three purposes: as an insurance policy, in case of either a deflationary or inflationary meltdown;

as a source of dry powder to purchase equities when their prices fall; and last, and certainly not least, to help you sleep at night. Since inflation is the greatest single threat to any bond portfolio, and since long-maturity bonds suffer the most in such a scenario, you should strive to keep the average maturities of your bonds well under five years.

Here, then, is what Yvonne's initial portfolio looks like:

- 25%   Vanguard Total Stock Market Index
- 25%   Vanguard Total International Index
- 50%   Vanguard Short-Term Bond Index

Table 6.4 displays her value averaging path. Every three months, she contributes $1,500 to her account—that is, $6,000 per year. The value averaging target for each of the stock funds increases by $375 each quarter, and for the bond fund, $750 each quarter. As explained earlier, this does not mean that she adds this precise amount to each fund. In the months when stocks do poorly, she will add more to the

Table 6.4 Young Yvonne's Value Averaging Target Amounts

	Total Stock Market	Total International	Short-Term Bond Index
1/1/2010	$375	$375	$750
4/1/2010	$750	$750	$1,500
7/1/2010	$1,125	$1,125	$2,250
10/1/2010	$1,500	$1,500	$3,000
1/1/2011	$1,875	$1,875	$3,750
4/1/2011	$2,250	$2,250	$4,500
7/1/2011	$2,625	$2,625	$5,250
10/1/2011	$3,000	$3,000	$6,000
1/1/2012	$3,375	$3,375	$6,750
4/1/2012	$3,750	$3,750	$7,500
7/1/2012	$4,125	$4,125	$8,250
10/1/2012	$4,500	$4,500	$9,000

stock funds to meet her targets, and vice versa. Whatever does not go into the stock funds will go into the bond or money market fund.

Further, Table 6.4 is only an example of what a value averaging path looks like. Because each of the Vanguard funds has a $3,000 minimum, this means that in practice she will not be able to own all three funds until she has accumulated at least $9,000, and she will not be able to achieve the proper 25/25/50 allocation until she has accumulated $12,000, which will not happen until she is two years into her savings plan.

Perhaps with the passage of time and with the accumulating savings, she will add in some more asset classes, such as a large-cap value fund, a small-cap value fund, or a REIT fund. But that is several years in her future. For now, she has her hands full working, saving, and executing her relatively simple plan.

Sheltered Sam (All Assets in Retirement Accounts)

Sam is a 50-year-old accountant somewhere in the Midwest; he is married and has four children. This disciplined professional has made "pay yourself first" the guiding principle of his financial life by assigning his IRA first crack at his paycheck. Because he is sending four kids through college, even with his family's modest lifestyle, he has accumulated little in taxable savings beyond a six-month emergency fund. Consequently, nearly all of his $500,000 nest egg sits in tax-sheltered retirement accounts, just like Yvonne's.

This is both a blessing and a curse. On the positive side, his account will compound tax-free for the next two to four decades, which should offset the higher tax rates. He will also be able to rebalance his asset classes without worrying about capital gains taxes. Best of all, like Yvonne, he has a very large proportion of sheltered assets, so he will be able to own any asset class he wants without worrying about its so-called tax efficiency—that is, how much ordinary income and capital gains it throws off.

On the minus side, he is going to take a big tax jolt when he retires and begins drawing down his IRA. Further, because of the nation's poor fiscal condition, it is highly likely that tax rates will be higher—perhaps much higher—then than they are now. Also, he will have to comply with the minimum required distributions from his accounts after reaching age 70½.

Sam lost a few nights of sleep over the equity market collapse of 2008–2009, but he did not panic and sell, so let's call his risk tolerance average. The formula arrived at in Chapter 2 (bond allocation = age, adjust for risk tolerance) assigns him a 50/50 stock/bond allocation. The following shows what his investment plan might look like. He will hold all of these positions, except for the final one—the taxable money market—in his IRA:

10%	Vanguard Large-Cap Index
12%	Vanguard Value Index
3%	Vanguard Small-Cap Index
8%	Vanguard Small-Cap Value Index
4%	Vanguard REIT Index
2%	Vanguard European Stock Index
2%	Vanguard Pacific Stock Index
3%	Vanguard Emerging Markets Index
3%	iShares MSCI Value Index
3%	Vanguard All-World ex-US Small-Cap Index (or ETF)
25%	Vanguard Short-Term Investment Grade Bond
20%	Vanguard Inflation-Protected Securities
5%	Money Market (taxable)

Getting his retirement account out of the local, full-service brokerage account was one of the hardest things Sam ever had to do. His broker, who he had known since second grade, was a fellow Rotarian and had coached his boys' T-ball teams. However, Sam knew that he was losing at least 2 percent per year in fees, commissions, and transactional costs to the brokerage firm, and that continuing to do so would jeopardize his and his wife's old age. Fortunately, his brokerage accounts were already split 50/50 between stocks and bonds, so he did not need to value average: Switching to the above strategy resulted in little dislocation of his desired asset allocation.

Because Sam has a relatively large amount of assets, he can afford to own a few extra bond asset classes as well. He has chosen to hold, for example, some inflation-protected bonds, that should also do at least tolerably well in any scenario, especially an inflationary one.

Taxable Ted (All Assets in a Taxable Account)

Like Yvonne, life has given Ted some hard knocks. Raised in the projects, he took the traditional route up available in our society to the poor but talented. He enrolled in engineering school, paid for by a part-time job. In Ted's case, this involved bouncing at a local nightclub, which provided a metaphor for the rest of his professional life, a succession of 80-hour work weeks filled with parts shortages, labor difficulties, unceasing travel, payroll squeezes, and, their inevitable consequence, two divorces. After nearly a quarter century on this treadmill, he had had it, and when a larger competitor offered Ted a seven-figure buyout, he did not need to be asked twice.

Since he never had the chance to save, let alone fund an IRA, Ted's now sitting on top of a large amount of entirely taxable cash. What should he do with it? Because of tax considerations, he is essentially limited to three stock asset classes: the large-cap U.S. markets, large-cap foreign markets, and U.S. small-cap stocks.

While he would like to own some value stocks, the opportunities to do so in a taxable account are limited. Dimensional

Fund Advisors does offer so-called "tax-managed" value funds, but these are available only through an advisor, and with his even temperament and quantitative skills, Ted feels he does not need one. He has also heard that ETFs might possibly be more tax-efficient than regular open-end funds, but the plain fact of the matter is that ETFs have really never been tested in this regard, because of large inflows and the low returns of the past decade.

He would also like to own REITs, and here an option is available: a variable annuity (VA). In general, VAs come wrapped in enormous fees and are offered by insurance companies, that as a group constitute some of the worst players in the financial business. Ideally, four conditions must be met for VA purchase: the investor should be relatively young—say, under 50; the investment should be in a highly tax-inefficient asset class; there should be no other sheltered accounts available to put them in; and finally, a low-cost passive vehicle in that asset class should be available in the VA. In fact, Vanguard does offer a relatively low-cost VA with an indexed REIT fund, and Ted should consider it.

Ted lives in California, and since his portfolio is subjected to hefty state and federal taxes, he has decided to split his bond portfolio four ways: a California intermediate-term municipal bond fund, a national municipal bond fund, a corporate bond fund, and a money market fund.

Let's discuss each bond fund in turn. Since he is a California resident and subject to a high marginal tax rate, why does he not invest all his fixed-income stash in California municipal bonds? In the first place, although he has been working hard, he has noticed the state's fiscal problems. More generally, because downgrades and defaults can be state-specific, he needs to diversify his bond portfolio against such risks in the same way that he diversifies his stock portfolio. Further, the national municipal bond fund he has chosen, the Vanguard Limited-Term Tax-Exempt

Fund, has a relatively short average maturity and is thus less adversely affected by inflation and rising interest rates than the California fund, which has a longer average maturity.

The Short-Term Investment-Grade Bond Fund, which holds mainly corporate debt, is fully taxable at both the state and federal level, but its after-tax yield is still competitive with the municipal bond funds; it provides yet one more rung of diversification.

Finally, why so much cash (money market)? I normally recommend a healthy dollop of short-term Treasury notes in place of cash, but Treasury yields are currently so low that it is better to put the funds in a money market account until short-term Treasury yields rise above 3 to 4 percent. Smaller investors might consider CDs in their place, but Ted's portfolio is too large to make these vehicles—with their $250,000 FDIC guarantee limit—practicable.

Finally, Ted has to decide his overall stock-bond mix. You might think that Ted has more than demonstrated his appetite for risk with his career choice, and you just might be right. There is only one problem: Like Yvonne, Ted's a financial virgin and has never invested through a bear market. Recall the difference between a flight-simulator crash and an actual crash: looking at a 25 percent loss in a spreadsheet and actually seeing your investment dollars—as Fred Schwed put it, "a real chunk of money that you used to own"—disappear are two entirely different things.

Because of Ted's inexperience with stocks, he is only going with a 40/60 stock/bond split. Besides, Ted has stashed away more than enough of a nest egg to retire on, so why should he take unnecessary risks? Here is what his portfolio might look like:

16%   Vanguard Total Stock Market Index
10%   Vanguard Tax-Managed Small-Cap
8%   Vanguard Tax-Managed International

> 2%   Vanguard Emerging Markets
> 4%   Vanguard REIT (Variable Annuity)
> 15%   Prime Money Market (later, individual Treasury Notes)
> 15%   California Intermediate-Term Tax-Exempt
> 15%   Limited-Term Tax-Exempt
> 15%   Short-Term Investment Grade

Finally, how does Taxable Ted deploy the proceeds of the sale of his company, which are currently in cash? This can be done in at least two different ways. The first would be a simple lump sum deployment, in which he purchases all of his stock and bond positions at once. At current stock valuations, this might be a reasonable thing to do.

Alternatively, Ted might set up a value averaging path for the risky stock assets in his proposed portfolio over the next several years. A compromise between the two techniques would be to invest the first half of his stock allocation right away, then value average the rest. Exactly which path Ted chooses depends upon his comfort level with the initial purchase of such a large amount of stocks.

In-Between Ida (Assets Divided Between Retirement and Taxable Accounts)

Ida presents a more difficult case than Sam or Ted. She has just been widowed at age 70. Her late husband Joe left her with a $1 million portfolio, a mix of taxable assets and retirement accounts, plus the payoff from Joe's life insurance policy.

The two of them had invested through no less than five bear markets between 1973 and 2008 (1973–1974, 1987, 1990, 2000–2002, and the most recent meltdown), so equity volatility does not faze her. When Joe retired at 65, he wisely chose to spend down some of their assets so as to postpone taking Social Security until his 70th birthday, which was just before he passed away.

In spite of his death just after starting Social Security, this was a brilliant decision. It increased Ida's monthly Social Security payment, which she will receive as his surviving spouse, by more than one-third, and is nearly double what it would have been had he chosen to start payments at age 62.

Ida will have to live to about 82 to make starting Social Security at age 70 "pay off," and if she fails to do so, then you might say that her husband had made the "wrong" choice. But remember Pascal's Wager! If Ida lives into her 90s (did I forget to tell you that both of her parents nearly became centenarians?), she will be very glad indeed for the extra $8,000 per year she'll get for waiting until age 70 to start payments.

Joe did not enjoy travel, and now Ida wants to kick up her heels a bit in Europe and Asia while she still enjoys good health; she figures she will need about $38,000 per year on top of her $30,000 annual Social Security income to pay for her $68,000 in annual living expenses, travel, and taxes. What should she do?

She is beginning with $500,000 in IRAs and $500,000 in taxable money and is tempted to take the entire $500,000 IRA account and purchase an inflation-adjusted immediate annuity that would pay her the $38,000 she needs to supplement her Social Security payments until she dies and split her policies among three highly rated insurance companies in order to diversify herself against the failure of one of them.

The trouble is this might not be such a great idea at the present time. It would be wonderful if American citizens could privately purchase additional annuity coverage equivalent to that offered by Social Security. Superficially, this seems to be the case. For example, many insurers offer inflation-adjusted annuities yielding a 6 percent annualized inflation-adjusted payout for a man and wife (7 percent for a single person) for 70-year-old annuitants, which an investor would not be able to sustain for more than one or two decades on his or her own.

Two years ago, the finest minds in retirement finance would have thought that annuitizing away Ida's "longevity risk" with annuity policies from several different insurance companies was a dandy idea. It never would have occurred to even the most prescient of them that, by 2008, the long-term survival of most of the insurance companies offering these products might be at risk.

The recent crisis has made painfully clear that the financial stability of the insurers themselves is not a sure thing. In my opinion, it would not be wise at this point to trust any insurance company, or combination of them, to stick around for the 20- to 40-year time horizon of a long-lived retiree.

In light of this, probably the smartest thing for Ida to do would be to delay annuitizing for at least several years in order to obtain some clarity about the long-term prospects of the insurance companies. In the meantime, she should invest the funds earmarked for her annuity in high-grade, short-term bond funds. Perhaps by the time she is 80 the government might get into the business of insuring commercial annuities, or even begin selling them itself.

This is not as far-fetched as it might seem; more than four centuries ago, both the Dutch and French governments financed their debt with annuities, and a modern-day version of this would provide a huge market for the burgeoning government debt. Further, absent the need to show a profit, the government would be able to offer an "actuarially fair" annuity with a significantly higher payout than those offered commercially. According to William Gale, director of the Retirement Studies Project at the Brookings Institution, the recent market meltdown has convinced investors that secure retirement income is at least as important as investment return, and may result in an FDIC-like agency to insure retirees against insurance company failure.[3]

Even if the situation does not improve by the time she becomes an octogenarian, Ida has eliminated 10 years of insurance company survival risk and can by that point collect an approximately 10 to 11 percent inflation-adjusted annuity payout.

Being highly risk-tolerant and needing only $38,000 extra per year, which is less than 4 percent of her portfolio, she has decided on a 50/50 stock/bond allocation. Here is how she will divide it:

10%	Vanguard Total Stock Market (Taxable)
8%	Vanguard Value Index (IRA)
3%	Vanguard Tax-Managed Small Cap (Taxable)
6%	Vanguard Small-Cap Value (IRA)
5%	Vanguard REIT (IRA)
5%	Vanguard Tax-Managed International (Taxable)
6%	iShares MSCI Value Index (IRA)
3%	Vanguard Emerging Markets (Taxable)
4%	Vanguard International Small-Cap Index (IRA)
20%	Vanguard Short-Term Investment-Grade Bond (IRA)
15%	Vanguard Limited-Term Tax-Exempt Bond (Taxable)
10%	Vanguard Ohio Tax-Exempt Bond (Taxable)
5%	Money Market (4% in Taxable, 1% in IRA)

Again, does this seem too aggressive for a 70-year-old? Only if you consider her portfolio in isolation. In reality, her $30,000 annual Social Security income is a "super-TIPS," whose coupon rises *faster* than the rate of inflation and could reasonably be valued at around $400,000 ($30,000 divided by a 7 percent inflation-adjusted annuity payout at age 70).

Since her Social Security payments rise with inflation, she did not include any TIPS in her portfolio. Thus, her portfolio allocation can reasonably be considered to be $500,000 in stocks and $900,000 in "bonds," or 36/64.* Finally, Ida should not reinvest the dividends in her taxable portfolio in order to build up her cash pad for emergencies.

The Rebalancing Question

Almost as soon as Yvonne, Sam, Ted, and Ida begin saving and investing, their portfolios will get out of whack. Consider a simple 50/50 portfolio established on December 31, 2007 consisting of $50,000 each Vanguard Total Stock Market and Vanguard Total Bond Market. By December 31, 2008 the stock fund was worth only $31,500, while the bond fund was worth $52,550. In order to reestablish the 50/50 allocation, the investor would have had to exchange $10,525 from the bond fund to the stock fund.

Before approaching the question of how to rebalance, we have to confront the elephant in the rebalancing room: taxes. Investors rebalance portfolios for two reasons: to enhance return and to reduce risk. The excess returns generated by rebalancing are not large, usually no greater than 1 percent per year, which is much smaller than the capital gains taxes you will realize on most sales. So purely from a returns point of view, you should never sell stocks to rebalance inside a taxable portfolio. Buying is fine, of course, and you can also use fund distributions—the capital gains, dividends, and interest the funds throw off—to rebalance as well.

---

*Care should be taken in capitalizing Social Security, annuity, and pension payments in this manner. In Ida's case, her $1.4 million portfolio of stocks, bonds, and capitalized Social Security payments should be applied to her full $68,000 in living expenses. Alternatively, if she only wishes to address her $38,000 in living expenses after Social Security, then it would not be proper to add her $400,000 in capitalized Social Security payments to her $1.0 million in stocks and bonds, since her monthly Social Security checks are already spoken for.

At some point, however, some selling is advisable to control risk. If you start with a 50/50 portfolio and a prolonged bull market takes your portfolio to 65/35, or even 75/25, then something needs to be done. So purely from a risk-control point of view, it is probably prudent to take the capital gains whenever the stock allocation gets to be more than 10 percent over policy and put the proceeds in the bond portion.

Of our four investors, this problem significantly affects only Taxable Ted. Sheltered Sam and Young Yvonne, with their nearly all-sheltered portfolios, do not have to worry about it at all. In-between Ida can easily do most of her rebalancing inside her sheltered account. Even if she needs to rebalance and sell some of an asset class in her taxable account, she can compensate with a closely related one on the sheltered side. For example, at some point Ida may need to sell some Large-Cap Market Fund. Instead of selling it and incurring a capital gain in her taxable account, she could sell some Value Index Fund from her IRA, which behaves very similarly, and re-adjust her allocations accordingly. If she is particularly clever, if it becomes necessary to buy more Large-Cap Index Fund, or any other fund on the taxable side, she can do it instead in her IRA so it can be sold free of capital gains on the next rebalancing round.

Having discussed the problems that rebalancing can create with taxes, just how, and how often, should you rebalance? The answer is relatively infrequently. It turns out that stock and asset class price changes are not *perfectly* random. Over periods of a year or less, prices do tend to "trend" a little bit: If a given asset class had better-than-average performance last month, there is a *slightly* better than average chance it also will next month; the same is true of less-than-average performance as well.

Rebalance your portfolio approximately once every few years; more than once per year is probably too often. In taxable portfolios, do so even less frequently.

Over periods of more than a year, the opposite occurs. Prices tend to "mean revert": An asset class with an above-average past return will tend, ever so slightly, to have a below-average future return, and vice versa. In sheltered accounts, the optimal strategy would seem to be to let the losses and gains run for two to three years, then rebalance. So an effective rebalancing interval would seem to be "every few years."

Do not underestimate the difficulty of adhering to this process, which from time to time takes industrial-grade discipline, particularly when making purchases in the face of potential economic catastrophe.

The most difficult question facing investors today is what to do after the recent overwhelming market decline. For young investors in the saving phase and small portfolio size relative to their human capital—that is, their future earnings—the path is clear: Stay the course, adhere to policy, and keep purchasing equities at cheap prices to maintain the proper stock/bond allocation.

For retirees with no future income outside of Social Security, the situation is different. Rebalancing aggressively consumes the bond portion of a portfolio, which the retiree draws from if equities head lower or do not recover from current levels for a prolonged period.

Consider the case of a 75-year-old investor with a $1 million portfolio that had been allocated 50/50 between stocks and bonds, but because of market declines is now 34/66. If he needs to withdraw $50,000 per year to meet living expenses, then the bonds in his portfolio, and the interest they throw off, will sustain him for about 11 years. Clearly, he is in Pascal's Wager territory: While he might reasonably believe that stock returns over the next decade or so will be high, if he rebalances aggressively, this will deplete his bond portfolio and reduce his 11-year margin of safety. If he is wrong and stocks do not do well for a decade, then plowing yet more of his bonds into equities will have lost him the wager, the consequences of which will be far more serious than the forgone higher returns of aggressive rebalancing if stock returns are high.

Finally, the rebalancing question illustrates yet one more advantage of an indexed/passive approach to investing. When an index fund does terribly, it is because that asset class has done terribly, which usually means that it has gotten cheaper. In turn, this usually means that its expected future returns have gone up, and that the investor can buy some more of the fund with a reasonably clean conscience. On the other hand, when an actively managed fund does terribly, the possibility that the poor performance is due to the manager's lack of skill gnaws at your self-confidence: Should you really be buying more of a fund run by a possibly incompetent manager? Did you make the wrong choice in the first place? Quite often, such poor performance is due to some combination of bad luck and poor asset-class performance. This may lead to the wrong decision: firing the fund manager just as his or her asset class is about to turn around or his or her luck is about to change. In short, indexing your investments means never having to say you're sorry.

Math Detail: Rebalancing, Momentum, and Mean Reversion

Recall the U.S. Large Stock/REIT portfolio from Chapter 3, and how an extra return was earned by rebalancing it back to policy each year—what I call the "rebalancing bonus." Are there some asset classes that produce a large bonus? Yes, there are. More than a decade ago I noticed that asset classes with particularly high volatility, such as precious metals equity, earned significantly higher internal rates of return (IRR, which is the same as dollar-weighted return) when rebalanced back to policy than the underlying asset-class, or fund, returns. I eventually derived a series of

(Continued)

(Continued)

equations that accurately predicted this gap. Those who are interested are encouraged to consult the work that mathematician David Wilkinson and I have done in this regard.[4]

The long and the short of it is that the three inputs to these equations are exactly the same as Markowitz's: returns, SDs, and correlations. In particular, the bonus is increased by high asset class volatility, low correlation, and equality of returns among asset classes.

With high volatility, the investor is buying lower and selling higher. Low correlation means that one asset is zigging more often when the other is zagging, so the investor is rebalancing more often.

But what really determines whether rebalancing increases returns or not is the similarity of returns. Consider another rebalancing pair, the S&P 500 and Japanese stocks for the decade between 1990 and 1999. During this period, the former returned 18.21 percent per year, while the latter actually lost 0.85 percent per year. Had an investor started with a 50/50 portfolio on January 1, 1990 and never rebalanced it, it would have earned an annualized return of 12.07 percent as U.S. stocks soared into the stratosphere while Japanese stocks deteriorated almost year after year. Had an investor rebalanced this portfolio annually, it would have earned only 9.14 percent, as the investor threw away good U.S. stocks after bad Japanese ones, year after year.

As this example shows, rebalancing can lose as well as gain return. Is there any reason to believe that, on average, rebalancing will help more than hurt? Not if we believe that market movements are random. After all, we rebalance with the hope that an asset with past higher/lower than average returns will have future lower/higher than average returns.

Is this actually true? Probably. Recall that over short periods of time asset classes demonstrate momentum, but that over periods longer than a year, they tend to mean-revert. Since momentum occurs over short periods, there are a lot of data points to look at, so providing statistical evidence for it has been easy for financial economists. Most financial economists consider stock and asset class momentum a fact of life, not to mention a direct challenge to the EMH.

Establishing that mean reversion exists, which is pretty much the same thing as showing that rebalancing yields, on average, a net benefit, proves much more difficult, since there are far fewer long periods. Consider the U.S. equity markets, for example, for which high-quality data exist only since 1925. If we want to look at mean reversion over five-year time horizons, we only have 16 independent periods to look at. (It is not kosher to look at overlapping periods.) Most financial economists and practitioners do believe that equities mean revert, but we will probably never know for sure.[5]

Besides the calendar-based strategies discussed above, the investor can employ a so-called "threshold" strategy by rebalancing at preset allocations above or below policy. This, unfortunately, is a very tricky proposition, and I have seen a lot of foolishness written on the topic. For example, some advisors suggest that asset classes be rebalanced when they get, say, 3 percent above or below their targets in absolute terms. This means that you would never do a rebalancing buy for any asset class with a 3 percent or less allocation. A more sophisticated approach would be to set proportionate limits, say, 20 percent above or below the target allocation. With the Value Index Fund's 12 percent allocation in Sam's policy, this would mean buying and selling at a 9.6 and 14.4 percent allocation, respectively.

There are three problems with this. First, because of the approximately lognormal distribution of asset class returns, a 20 percent relative rise in price is more likely than a 20 percent fall. In lognormal terms, a 20 percent rise counterbalances, and is equally likely as, a 16.67 percent fall. Second, some asset classes are more volatile than others; set a 20 percent threshold for U.S. large cap stocks, and you will hit it every year or two. With emerging markets, you will be trading much more frequently. Finally, the thresholds will have to be portfolio-specific; using a fixed threshold in an all-stock portfolio will result in far fewer rebalances because all stock asset classes move together than in a nearly all-bond portfolio, where the stock moves relative to the bonds will be much larger.

Which is better, calendar or threshold rebalancing? It is impossible to determine, since the benefits of rebalancing are not much

(Continued)

(Continued)

greater than 1 percent per year; proving that one method was better than another would mean statistically powering the test to detect differences in return of perhaps one or two dozen basis points, which would probably take hundreds or even thousands of years of data.

Because of these complexities, I recommend that beginners stick to rebalancing by the calendar once every few years or so. If at some point you do decide to switch to the threshold technique, you will need to develop individual rebalancing parameters that are not only asset-class specific, but also portfolio-specific as well. Threshold rebalancing for most practitioners tends to be a work in progress. Rebalancing a given asset class too often or too infrequently is usually a signal to adjust the threshold up or down, respectively.

Teach Your Children Well

For young parents, there is a financial goal far more important than saving for their own retirement: their children's financial future.

Job one in financial child rearing is inoculating your offspring against the corrosive effects of our modern brand-name consumer society. If as children they are overly focused on the latest in sneakers, clothes, and cell phones, then as adults they will lust after the fanciest autos and the biggest houses, usually with disastrous effects. Go out of your way to disdain these things, and when as teenagers they point out that their friends' parents seem to have more money than you do, inform them firmly that the only thing they know for sure is that these parents have *spent* more money than you have. It is perfectly acceptable, in my opinion, to imply that many of their friends' parents likely *owe* more money too. Establish a firm link between money and work by predicating their allowance on the completion of a discrete list of household chores.

If you are not leading by example in this endeavor, then do not even try; if you are visibly balancing mortgages and credit card balances to pay for vacations, eating out, a McMansion, and SUVs, then the game is lost, both for you and your progeny.

Jonathan Clements, who wrote about personal finance issues for many years and has raised two children, frequently weighed in on the subject in his column in *the Wall Street Journal.* One of his primary insights was the negative role played by the "Bank of Mom and Dad": the endless supply of five dollar bills emanating from your wallet for your kids' casual needs. Mr. Clements offers two very useful tips for breaking this cycle:

1. Encourage frugality by rewarding it. For example, pay your children a dollar each time they order ice water in a restaurant instead of a soda.
2. As soon as they are old enough to handle an ATM card—say, 11 or 12—break the link to the Bank of Mom and Dad by depositing their allowance into a bank account. When the money's gone, it's gone. Soon enough, they will learn to treasure a warm fuzzy reserve balance.[6]

Next, teach your children to invest. I suggest that at age 10 you set up a small portfolio with two or three mutual funds in each child's name. Teach them how to file their account statements and/or to log on and print out reports. Each quarter, schedule an investment meeting with all the involved siblings and discuss portfolio performance. Reward them for these chores with the dividends from the money market or bond funds, and with half the capital appreciation of the stock funds.

The most important financial bequest to your heirs will not be cold hard cash, but rather the ability to save, spend, and invest prudently.

They will get to observe up close the different behavior of various asset classes. With any amount of luck, they will experience a severe bear market in the process and lose the equivalent of several months' or years' allowance in one fell swoop. This is your chance to teach them the following message:

> It's OK to lose money in stocks as long as this is the result of overall market declines. Never be sorry when it happens; this is the price that you must pay for longer-term high returns. In fact, a very wise and famous man once said that it was the duty of investors to lose money from time to time.[7]

Fifteen years ago, when I began writing finance books, finding funds with low minimums for this purpose was easy, especially for childrens' accounts. This is no longer the case; for example, Vanguard has raised its minimums on almost all its funds to at least $3,000. But there are still some decent choices for this purpose such as the Oakmark family, which offers a value-oriented approach to foreign and domestic equities with a $1,000 minimum.

Summary

Of course, Yvonne, Sam, Ted, and Ida are only starting points. Whatever else you do, do not take a cookie-cutter approach to your retirement nest egg. You will need to take into consideration several factors in designing your investment policy:

- How much complexity can I handle? Some investors are asset-class junkies, happy with upwards of 20 different asset classes, and thus 20 different mutual funds, while others will throw up their hands at an account with more than four or five mutual funds. Did Sheltered Sam's portfolio give you a headache?

Better stick with just three asset classes/funds: one each for the total U.S. stock market, the international stock markets, and the bond market.

- What are my personal asset class preferences? The prospect of inflation terrifies some investors, and so they seek shelter in precious metals—either gold and silver coins or the shares of mining companies—while others shy away from investing in emerging markets that have poor shareholder protection, undrinkable water, and regular military coups. While investing competency requires emotional self-control, you do need to sleep at night, and in the long run precisely what asset classes you include or omit—and their exact proportions—will prove far less important than your ability to stick to your plan.

- How much "tracking error" can I tolerate? Whether you want to admit it or not, you are going to be comparing your investment results, if only tacitly, to those of your family and friends, who on average will be investing largely in a portfolio that looks very much like the large-growth-heavy S&P 500 or Wilshire 5000. If you choose to emphasize value stocks, small stocks, or foreign stocks, I can guarantee that there will be periods like the late 1990s when this approach seriously underperforms that of your neighbors. For example, in 1998, the S&P 500 returned over 28 percent, yet it was quite possible to assemble a value-, small-, and foreign-heavy portfolio that *lost* money in that year. Worse, in 2008, while the S&P 500 lost "only" 37 percent, small, value, REIT, and foreign stocks did much worse. Will you be willing to tolerate such short-term relative disasters in the hope that they will *probably* yield higher returns in the long run? If the answer is no, then you had better stick with a simpler total-stock market-focused portfolio à la Taxable Ted.

- How do I adjust for my human capital? Whether you know it or not, there is quite a bit of value locked up inside you that needs to be integrated with your financial assets. For example, do you work for a large "value" corporation that is extremely sensitive to the health of the nation's economy? If you do, then do not load up on value stocks. On the other hand, if you are a bankruptcy lawyer, letter carrier, or plumber, then be my guest. Do you receive a large monthly pension or disability check, or enough from Social Security to meet most of your living expenses? Then in actuality, you own far more "bonds" than you think. For example, assume that you are getting $30,000 per year from Social Security. As we saw with In-Between Ida, the present value of all those future checks is $30,000 divided by 7 percent, or about $400,000. If your personal nest egg was approximately $200,000, some might reasonably argue that you could invest *all* of it in stocks, since it would constitute just 33 percent of your actual net worth (that is, $200,000 of the $600,000 total of your liquid assets and present value of your Social Security). I would not recommend doing this, but if you can comfortably live on your Social Security checks, there would be nothing wrong with investing most of your personal nest egg in stocks, since in reality you are investing for your heirs.
- Never forget that the portfolio's the thing: Inevitably, it will contain poorly performing asset classes—there will always be at least *one*—but its identity will change from year to year. It is the overall return of the portfolio that counts.
- No matter how you allocate your assets, you will always wish that you had assigned more to the best performer and nothing at all to the worst performer.

Since no one can predict which these will be, the safest course is to own them all, and thereby, as best you can, assure yourself of not being devastated by an Enron or a Lehman. When you minimize your expenses and diversify, you forego bragging rights with the neighbors and in-laws, but you will also minimize the chances of impoverishing yourself and the ones you love.

And that, ladies and gentlemen, is one fair trade.

CHAPTER

The Name of the Game

Over the past three decades, the powers that be have handed investors, particularly those saving for retirement, a very raw deal indeed. First and foremost, the traditional pension plan, which in the past had provided tens of millions of ordinary American workers with a secure income and a dignified retirement, has been replaced with an investment mess of pottage: poorly designed, overly expensive, and thus miserably performing defined-contribution plans that seem almost consciously designed to fail.

Worse, the average American is assumed to somehow possess the expertise and, more importantly, the emotional discipline to execute a competent lifetime investment plan, a goal that even many Wall Street professionals fall well short of. In the coming decades, retirees, and our society as a whole, will reap the whirlwind of this folly.

The nation is only slowly beginning to wake up to the enormity of the situation, and it will not be remedied any time soon. In the meantime, I hope I have provided you with the tools to personally avoid becoming a casualty of this looming catastrophe.

Needless to say, you have a great deal of skin in this game. If you bypass this book's advice and make all of the classic investment mistakes—ignoring expenses, chasing hot asset classes and managers, underestimating your risk tolerance, and being overly swayed by your family, friends, neighbors, and the news—you will almost certainly join the millions of Americans doomed to a quiet life of retirement desperation. On the other hand, if you take the advice between these covers and keep expenses to a minimum with a prudent mix of index funds and keep your head while everyone else is losing theirs, then you will at least have a fighting chance.

Toward this end, I have enumerated several skill sets that every competent investor should master. Tie them together into lists that could be stuck to your refrigerator. Grab your breakfast, look regularly at these lists, and embrace this manifesto.

Investment Theory and History: The Short Course

❑ First and foremost, risk and return are intimately related. You cannot earn high returns without bearing painful losses along the way. You cannot achieve perfect safety without condemning yourself to low, long-term returns. The promise of high returns with low risk is a reliable indicator of fraud.

❑ From time to time, the markets can go stark raving mad, as occurred on the upside in the 1990s, or on the downside during the 1930s and the past two years. Your primary defense against being swept up in the madness of such periods is a command of the history of the financial markets and the resulting ability to say, "I've been here before, and I know how the story ends."

❑ History also provides some guidance about the risks of stocks and bonds. However, the ability to deploy the Gordon Equation in order to estimate future returns is even more valuable. For stocks, this is as simple as adding the dividend yield of the market to its expected per-share growth rate; for bonds, subtract the default rate from the interest rate. Both of these will provide reasonably accurate forecasts of long-term results. At present, this analysis suggests a 4 to 8 percent real return for various classes of stocks, a 2 percent real return for corporate bonds, and a somewhat negative real return for government bonds, especially at short maturities.

❑ Never forget that at the level of individual securities, the markets are brutally efficient. Whenever you buy or sell an individual stock or bond, you are likely trading with someone who is smarter and better informed than you are, and who is working harder at it. In the worst case scenario, you are competing against a corporate executive who knows more about his or her company than even the best analyst. You are as likely to win this game as you are to star in the next Spielberg movie.

The Portfolio Theory of Everything

❑ The primary decision facing you, the investor, is the overall percentages of the portfolio allotted to stocks and bonds; this determines the risk-return characteristics of the mix.

❑ Since we cannot predict in advance which stock and bond asset classes will perform the best, we diversify. During periods of sharp market declines, all stock asset classes tend to drop, but in the long run, diversification among stock asset classes often works quite well, thank you.

❑ The portfolio's the thing; do not pay too much attention to its best and worst performing asset classes.

We Have Met the Enemy, and He Is Us

❑ You are your own worst investment enemy, and your most grievous sin is likely to be overconfidence. Do not imagine for one minute that you are able to successfully pick stocks and mutual funds, or that you are able to time the market.

❏ Investors tend to be too susceptible to the emotional impact of the news and to the fear and greed of their neighbors. The better you can tune out this emotional noise, the wealthier you will be. Conversely, if you find yourself owning the same securities as your friends and neighbors, you are likely doing something wrong.

❏ Human beings are pattern-seeking primates. Most of what goes on in the financial markets, by contrast, is random noise. Avoid imagining patterns; there usually are none.

Heads I Win, Tails You Lose

❏ Stockbrokers service their clients in the same way that Baby Face Nelson serviced banks. The more they charge you in fees and commissions and the more disreputable the products they sell you, the higher their income will be. Most likely, they were attracted to the brokerage business for the same reasons that Mr. Nelson and Willie Sutton were attracted to banks— because it is where the money is. Avoid full-service brokerage houses at all costs.

❏ Most mutual funds are not much better; their primary goal is not to invest well, but rather to gather assets. These are two entirely different things. Choose fund companies that are owned by the fund shareholders themselves, or are at least privately owned. Avoid fund companies that are owned by publicly traded parent firms.

Fire When Ready

❏ You should live as modestly as you can and save as much as you can for as long as you can. Saving too much is not nearly as harmful as saving too little.

❑ Design your overall stock/bond allocation with your age and risk tolerance firmly in mind.

❑ Consider tilting toward small and value stocks, since they will likely have higher expected returns than the overall market. Precisely how much you do so depends upon the nature of your employment and your tolerance for temporarily underperforming the market for up to several years.

❑ If you need to spend more than 4 percent of your nest egg in retirement per year, seriously consider purchasing an immediate fixed annuity. However, you should delay doing this until after the current economic crisis has passed and the status of issuing insurance companies becomes clearer. In any case, the best "annuity purchase" you can make is to delay beginning Social Security until age 70.

❑ Teach your children well; the most important financial bequest you make to your children will not be monetary, but rather their ability to save, invest, and spend prudently.

Finally, never, ever forget Pascal's Wager as it applies to investing: The name of the game is not to get rich, but rather to avoid dying poor. In fact, if you follow the advice in this book, I can guarantee you that you *will not* get fabulously wealthy. Rather, I've striven to simultaneously maximize your chances of a comfortable retirement and minimize your chances of living out your final years in poverty. I know of no more laudable or more worthy investment goal.

The Books You Need
... Aged Like Fine Wine

Concision has its price. I designed this book to illustrate how investors should respond to today's scary markets, and those who are just beginning their investment education will need to continue the learning process. As outlined here, there are four areas that every investor has to master: the theory, the history, the psychology, and the business of finance. I have provided what I hope is a reasonable taste of all four areas, but if you are serious about your investment future—and you would be insane not to be—you have much further to travel. The good news is that all of the reading I recommend is a genuine pleasure, crafted by writers whose prose goes down like fine claret.

Theory: Burton G. Malkiel's *A Random Walk Down Wall Street: The Best and Latest Investment Advice Money Can Buy* (W.W. Norton & Co., 2006) will walk you through everything you need to know about exactly how stocks, bonds, and portfolios behave and how you should approach them. Now in its ninth edition, you would do well to reread each new one as Professor Malkiel cranks them out.

History: Edward Chancellor's *Devil Take the Hindmost: A History of Financial Speculation* (Plume, 2000) remains the classic narrative on bubbles and panics.

One day—it might be next year or in 30 years—you will watch the financial markets go completely bonkers—either up or down—and say to yourself, thanks to Mr. Chancellor, "I've seen this movie, and I know how it ends." You just might leave him something in your will.

Psychology: Some time ago, Jason Zweig took a leave from his regular gig at *Money* magazine and followed his bliss into the area of neuroeconomics. The result of his efforts, *Your Money and Your Brain* (Simon and Schuster, 2007), is a delicious romp through the thicket of human nature and the havoc it wreaks on our finances.

Business: Long ago, I lost count of the number of incisive books Jack Bogle has written about the investment industry, but for my money his *Common Sense on Mutual Funds, Fully Updated 10th Anniversary Edition* (John Wiley & Sons, 2009) still provides the best roadmap through this jungle.

This book most definitely is not a personal finance guide. Although Jonathan Clements' *The Little Book of Main Street Money* (John Wiley & Sons, 2009) covers much the same ground as this title, it also contains the wisdom collected by one of the most prolific and perceptive financial writers on the planet about many nuts-and-bolts personal issues not covered here. If you have questions about debt management, balancing college savings and retirement needs, life insurance, the financial education of children, juggling retirement accounts—the list goes on and on—consult Jonathan's book.

Finally, if you are mathematically inclined and would like to deploy the value averaging technique described in the last chapter the way it was really meant to be done, Michael Edleson's *Value Averaging: The Safe and Easy Strategy for Higher Investment Returns* (John Wiley & Sons, 2006) will probably boost your long-term returns more than any other title on your shelf.

As I said repeatedly in this book, I am upbeat about future returns in the world's stock and bond markets. However, this optimism does not extend to the prospects for their successful exploitation by the millions of Americans dragooned into the retirement investing process—a process, I fear, whose primary outcome will be the transfer of yet more wealth from ordinary citizens to brokerage houses and mutual fund companies.

These books should enable you to avoid the pitfalls that more often than not sink the plans of most retirees. Always remember that investing is not a destination, but rather a journey of discovery and learning. With luck, you have just gotten a good start.

Notes

Preface

1. Ip, Greg, "The Bull Market May Be on the Ropes, But the Bull Mentality Acts Like a Champ," *Wall Street Journal* (Sept. 14, 1998).

Chapter 1: A Brief History of Financial Time

1. Sidney Homer and Richard Sylla, *A History of Interest Rates* (Hoboken, NJ: John Wiley & Sons, 2005), 17–54.
2. Roger G. Ibbotson and Gary P. Brinson, *Global Investing: The Professional's Guide to the World Capital Markets* (New York: McGraw-Hill, 1993), 149.
3. Homer and Sylla, 119.
4. John Julius Norwich, *A History of Venice* (New York: Alfred A. Knopf, 1982), 243–256.
5. James Grant, "Is the Medicine Worse Than the Illness?" *Wall Street Journal* (December 20, 2008).

Chapter 2: The Nature of the Beast

1. For a good review of this topic, see Elroy Dimson et al., *Triumph of the Optimists: 101 Years of Global Investment Returns* (Princeton NJ: Princeton University Press, 2002).
2. Nicholas Nassim Taleb, *The Black Swan: The Impact of the Highly Improbable* (New York: Random House, 2007).
3. William J. Bernstein and Robert D. Arnott, "The Two-Percent Dilution," *Financial Analysts Journal* 59, no. 5 (September–October 2003): 47–55.
4. Data from msci.com.
5. Irving Fisher, *The Theory of Interest* (New York: Macmillan, 1930), and John B. Williams, *The Theory of Investment Value* (Cambridge, MA: Harvard University Press, 1938). Williams usually receives credit for inventing the discounted dividend model, and indeed, he did work out its mathematics in much greater detail than Fisher. But Fisher clearly laid down its basic tenets.

6. Robert J. Shiller, "Long-Term Perspectives on the Current Boom in Home Prices," *Economists' Voice* 3, no. 4 (2006): 1–11.

7. Eugene F. Fama and Kenneth R. French, "The Cross-Section of Expected Stock Returns," *Journal of Finance* 47, no. 2 (June 1992): 427–465; Eugene F. Fama and Kenneth R. French, "Value versus Growth: The International Evidence," *Journal of Finance* 53, no 6 (December 1998): 1975-1999; and James L. Davis, Eugene F. Fama, and Kenneth R. French, "Characteristics, Covariances, and Average Returns: 1929 to 1997," *Journal of Finance* 55, no. 1 (February 2000): 389–406.

8. Daily price moves computed from Yahoo.com for the following funds: VFINX, DFLVX, DFSVX, VTGSX, and VGSIX, accessed March 1, 2009.

9. Annotated excerpts from David Leinweber, "Stupid Data Mining Tricks," slide presentation for First Quadrant Corporation, 1998.

10. Tom Lauricella, "The Stock Picker's Defeat," *Wall Street Journal* (December 10, 2008), C1.

11. William J. Bernstein, *The Four Pillars of Investing: Lessons for Building a Winning Portfolio,* (New York: McGraw-Hill, 2002), 84–85.

12. Nassim Nicholas Taleb, *Fooled by Randomness: The Hidden Role of Chance in Life and in the Markets, Second Edition* (New York: Random House, 2008).

13. John R. Graham and Campbell R. Harvey, "Grading the Performance of Market Timing Newsletters," *Financial Analysts Journal* 53, no. 6 (November–December 1997): 54–66.

14. John Bogle, email communication and *John Bogle on Investing: The First 50 Years* (New York: Mc-Graw Hill, 2000), 221–269, 335–400.

15. William Schultheis, *The Coffeehouse Investor: How to Build Wealth, Ignore Wall Street, and Get on with Your Life* (Atlanta, GA: Longstreet, 1998), 81–87.

Chapter 3: The Nature of the Portfolio

1. This statement is commonly attributed to Paul Samuelson, though I am unable to find a formal reference.

2. Social Security Online, http://www.ssa.gov/OACT/STATS/table4c6 .html, accessed April 1, 2009.

3. William J. Bernstein, *The Four Pillars of Investing: Lessons for Building a Winning Portfolio* (New York: McGraw-Hill, 2002), 101.

4. Ronald Surz, unpublished data via email, 2001.

5. Charles D. Ellis, *Winning the Loser's Game: Timeless Strategies for Successful Investing, Third Edition* (New York: McGraw-Hill, 1998), 101.

6. Ibid.

7. Fred Schwed, *Where Are the Customers' Yachts? or a Good Hard Look at Wall Street* (Hoboken, NJ: John Wiley & Sons, 2006), 54.

8. "The Death of Equities," *BusinessWeek* (August 13, 1979). The text of this article is available at http://www.fiendbear.com/deatheq.htm.

9. Harry Markowitz, "Portfolio Selection," *Journal of Finance* 7, no.1 (March 1952): 77–91.

Chapter 4: The Enemy in the Mirror

1. Jason Zweig, *Your Money and Your Brain: How the New Science of Neuroeconomics Can Help Make You Rich* (New York: Simon and Schuster, 2007).

2. For an excellent review of this topic, see Michael Marmot, *The Status Syndrome: How Social Standing Affects Our Health and Longevity* (New York: Times Books, 2004).

3. Kurt Vonnegut, *Cat's Cradle* (New York: Delta Trade Paperbacks, 1998), 182.

4. Andrew Coors and Lawrence Speidell, "Exuberant Irrationality: Judging Financial Books by their Covers," *Journal of Behavioral Finance* 7, no. 4 (2006):18–192.

5. For an excellent review of the fear/amygdala connection, see Elizabeth A. Phelps and Joseph E. LeDoux, "Contributions of the Amygdala to Emotional Processing: From Animal Models to Human Behavior," *Neuron* 48, no. 2 (October 20, 2005): 175–187.

6. Baba Shiv et al., "Investment Behavior and the Negative Side of Emotion," *Psychological Science* 16, no. 6 (June 2005): 435–439.

7. Shlomo Benzarti and Richard H. Thaler, "Myopic Loss Aversion and the Equity Premium Puzzle," *Quarterly Journal of Economics* 110, no. 1 (January 1995): 73-92.

8. Morgan Stanley Capital Indexes, www.mscibarra.com.

9. Philippe Jorion and William N. Goetzmann, "Global Stock Markets in the Twentieth Century," *Journal of Finance* 54, no. 3 (June, 1999): 953–980.

10. Jeremy Siegel, *Stocks for the Long Run: The Definitive Guide to Financial Market Returns & Long Term Investment Strategies* (New York: McGraw-Hill, 2007), 124–125; Bernstein and Arnott, Larry Speidell et al., "Dilution is a Drag . . . The Impact of Financings in Foreign Markets," *Journal of Investing* 14, no. 4 (Winter 2005): 17–22; Jay R. Ritter, "Economic Growth and Equity Returns: Conventional Wisdom is Wrong Again," working paper, November 1, 2004; Elroy Dimson, et al., *Triumph of the Optimists: 101 Years of Global Investment Returns* (Princeton, NJ: Princeton University Press, 2002), 156.

11. See Bernstein and Arnott, Speidell et al., and Ritter, op. cit.

12. Brian Knutson et al., "Distributed Neural Representation of Expected Value," *Journal of Neuroscience* 25, no. 16 (May 11, 2005): 4806–4812. See also Brian Knutson et al., "Anticipation of Increasing Monetary

Reward Selectively Recruits Nucleus Accumbens," *Journal of Neuroscience* 21, no. RC159 (2001): 1–5, and Patricio O'Donnell et al., "Modulation of Cell Firing in the Nucleus Accumbens," *Annals of the New York Academy of Sciences* 877 (Jun. 29, 1999): 157–175.

13. See Scott A. Huettel et al., "Perceiving Patterns in Random Series: Dynamic Processing of Sequence in Prefrontal Cortex," *Nature Neuroscience* 5, no. 5 (May 2002), 285–490. This paper demonstrates that the prefrontal cortex—just above our eyes—responds most strongly to the *breaking* of a pattern of events, even if it is only two events long. For example, if a subject is presented with A-A-A-B-A-A, fMRI will show prefrontal activation simultaneous with the "B."

14. Terry Odean, "What I Know About How You Invest," http://www .leggmason.com/billmiller/conference/illustrations/odean.asp, accessed March 15, 2009.

15. Barna Research, "Americans Describe Their Views About Life After Death," http://www.barna.org/barna-update/article/5-barna-update/ 128-americans-describe-their-views-about-life-after-death, accessed March 6, 2009.

16. Sarah Lubman and John R. Emshwiller, "Before the Fall: Hubris and Ambition in Orange County: Robert Citron's Story," *Wall Street Journal* (January 18, 1995), A1.

17. Karl Marx and Frederick Engles, *Selected Works*, 3 vols, bk 1 (Moscow: Progress Publishers, 1969), 163.

18. Niall Ferguson, *The Ascent of Money: A Financial History of the World* (New York: Penguin Press, 2008), 329–330.

19. Quoted in William Bernstein, *The Intelligent Asset Allocator: How to Build Your Portfolio to Maximize Returns and Minimize Risk* (New York: McGraw-Hill, 2000), 18.

20. Burton Malkiel, *A Random Walk Down Wall Street: The Time-Tested Strategy for Successful Investing* (New York: W.W. Norton, 2003), 24.

21. Jason Zweig, "Wall Street's Wisest Man," *Money* 30, no. 6 (June 2001).

Chapter 5: Muggers and Worse

1. John Rothchild, *A Fool and His Money* (New York, Viking Press, 1988), 145–155, quote from 147.

2. Quoted in Louis Lowenstein, *The Investor's Dilemma: How Mutual Funds Are Betraying Your Trust and What to Do* (Hoboken, NJ: John Wiley & Sons, 2008), 69.

3. Jason Zweig, http://www.jasonzweig.com/documents/speeches/Serving 2Masters.doc, accessed January 18, 2009. Mr. Zweig tells me that his audience, composed mainly of mutual fund executives, was less than appreciative of his message.

Chapter 6: Building Your Portfolio

1. Michael Edleson, *Value Averaging: The Safe and Easy Strategy for Higher Investment Returns* (Hoboken, NJ: John Wiley & Sons, 2006). Full disclosure: I'm such a big fan of this technique that I wrote the foreword for the latest edition. Beyond that, I have no financial connection with Dr. Michael Edleson, and certainly not with his current employer, Morgan Stanley.
2. William Bernstein, *The Four Pillars of Investing: Lessons for Building a Winning Portfolio* (New York: McGraw-Hill, 2002), 265–279.
3. Personal communication, Robert Gale.
4. See William Bernstein, "The Rebalancing Bonus," http://www.efficientfrontier.com/ef/996/rebal.htm, see also http://www.efficientfrontier.com/ef/197/rebal197.htm, http://www.efficientfrontier.com/ef/797/rebal797.htm, http://www.efficientfrontier.com/ef/100/rebal100.htm; and William J. Bernstein and David J. Wilkinson, "Diversification, Rebalancing, and the Geometric Mean Frontier," http://papers.ssrn.com/sol3/papers.cfm?abstract_id=53503.
5. For a good summary of the data in support of momentum, see, Andrew W. Lo and A. Craig MacKinlay, *A Non-Random Walk Down Wall Street* (Princeton, NJ: Princeton University Press, 1999); and for the difficulties of examining mean reversion, see Ronald Balvers et al., "Mean Reversion across National Stock Markets and Parametric Contrarian Investment Strategies," *Journal of Finance* 55, no. 2 (April 2000): 745–772.
6. I cannot recommend the column this advice came from enough. Jonathon Clements, "Bank of Mom and Dad," *Wall Street Journal*, http://online.wsj.com/article/SB119764562207829505.html.
7. Quoted in Bernstein, *The Intelligent Asset Allocator* (New York: McGraw-Hill, 2000), 18.

Acknowledgments

No author can tie together material from so many disparate areas—financial theory, financial history, psychology, and the nuts and bolts of the investment business—without a great deal of outside help. In addition, when someone begins a writing career later in life, large dollops of encouragement and advice are required.

To John Rekenthaler, Scott Burns, and Jonathan Clements: for taking the time more than a decade ago to supply advice and direction on the craft of financial writing, to say nothing of more than a few early breaks, to a total stranger. To Jack Bogle: who showed me, and millions of others, just how it's done. To Jason Zweig: for teaching this neurologist more than a thing or two about how our brains work, for his perspective on the business of investing, and for keeping me on my toes in general. To Susan Sharin, my partner in Efficient Frontier Advisors LLC: for providing me not only with the wisdom she accumulated over her decades in the business, but also for her eagle-eyed editing skills.

Abhishek Srinivasan and Jeff Cornell provided necessary data, while Wes Neff guided me through the pre-publication process. William Gale of the Brookings Institution walked me through the policy discussions surrounding retirement vehicles in the current administration. Meg Freeborn, Kevin Holm, and Bill Falloon, my editors at John Wiley & Sons, provided desperately needed guidance, advice, and polishing, while Ed Tower saved me from more than a few embarrassments; all remaining errors are mine alone.

Finally, to my wife, Jane Gigler, who devoted scores of hours of her precious time to this manuscript, turned unreadable jumbles of prose into coherent chapters, camouflaged my lack of literary training as best she could, and tolerated a distracted husband in the process. God knows where I would be without her.

About the Author

William **J. Bernstein**, PhD, MD, is a neurologist, cofounder of Efficient Frontier Advisors LLC, an investment management firm, and the editor of an asset allocation journal, *Efficient Frontier* (www.efficientfrontier.com). Bill is the bestselling author of four books: *The Intelligent Asset Allocator* and *The Four Pillars of Investing*, and two volumes of economic history, *The Birth of Plenty* and *A Splendid Exchange*. *The Intelligent Asset Allocator* and *The Four Pillars of Investing* are highly regarded, plain-spoken guides on how to build a diversified portfolio—without the help of a financial advisor. His columns appear regularly in *Money* magazine, and he has also written for *Barron's* financial magazine, *Mutual Funds* magazine, *American Medical News,* and Morningstar, Inc.

Index